WHAT HAVE WE HERE

ESSAYS ABOUT KEEPING HOUSE
AND FINDING HOME

SUSAN BONO

Tiny Lights Publications
P.O. Box 928
Petaluma, CA 94952
editor@tiny-lights.com

Manuscript Editor: Rebecca Lawton
Book Design: Ali Cross, Novel Ninjutsu
Cover Design and Art: Laurie MacMillan
Author Photo: Christine Paravicini
Word Cloud Image: Doug Fortier

ISBN-13: 978-0692279434 (Tiny Lights Publications)

For my family

May all our roads lead home

Cynthia —
May our paths
cross again —

♡ Susan
Emmndal
2018

My heart was a habitation large enough for many guests, but lonely and chill, and without a household fire. I longed to kindle one! It seemed not so wild a dream.

Nathaniel Hawthorne, *The Scarlet Letter* (1850)

CONTENTS

LETTING GO

ACKNOWLEDGEMENTS

RESOURCES AND LINKS

ABOUT THE AUTHOR

PREFACE

Iᴹ ʏᴏᴜ ᴀsᴋᴇᴅ ᴍᴇ ᴛᴏ ᴅʀᴀᴡ ᴀ ᴘɪᴄᴛᴜʀᴇ ᴏꜰ ᴀ ʜᴏᴜsᴇ, ɪ'ᴅ ᴜsᴇ ᴛʜᴇ time-tested formula I learned around age five. Joyce McKinley, a slightly older, more sophisticated neighbor, taught me to start with a rectangle. Next, add a door dead center, two windows above, a triangle for a roof, and a chimney with a curl of smoke forever rising. If I wanted to get fancy, I'd add tie-back curtains, a curving path, maybe a crayoned tree and a few tulips.

I've never really cared, then or now, that no real house looks like this. My disinterest in the facts may also explain why I grew up assuming the world was full of wasp-waisted women like the ones I watched on my family's black-and-white TV who kept house wearing high heels and pearls. Ignorance of this sort protects the part of me that has always wanted to keep everything about home simple, predictable, and recognizable at a distance.

But home is a mystery, like dawn, or twilight, or a landscape wrapped in fog. Sometimes it's a refuge, sometimes a prison. It lives in the untended garden, the scent of sheets on a waiting bed, conversations around the dinner table, and all that goes unsaid. Home is a mirror, a window, a beacon. Its roots run deep and are tangled in love, habit, dysfunction, and longing. Home is a place I build and destroy every day, a place where I belong, yet am always leaving. It's the "You are Here" on all my maps. It changes shape every time I look at it.

I never thought much about home when I was a kid. I didn't

have to. Mine was always there, a carefully tended, one-bathroom ranch house on Helen Way in Woodland, California, where my parents, brother, and cat lived, my clothes hung in a closet, and meals, family, and Santa always arrived on time. During my early years at Dingle Elementary School, I dreamed of traveling the world as an archeologist, or maybe an actress. This meant my home might be a tent, a grand hotel, or a backstage dressing room. Nothing permanent. In sixth grade, when classmate Peggy Ackley invited me to write a story she would illustrate about a girl and her pet mouse, I imagined growing up to be a writer, but always in exotic locations, like a Parisian garret or a train compartment.

Instead, my path led to college at San Francisco State and a career as a high school English teacher. In 1980, I married my college sweetheart and moved to Petaluma, a small Northern California town very much like the farming community I grew up in, and only ninety miles away. When our first son was born in 1985, I left teaching to be a full-time mom. With a husband, family, and a house, I had everything I needed to root me to the spot.

Staying home with babies brought about a somewhat predictable blend of satisfaction and madness. Even as I counted my blessings, I was plagued with questions about who I was and what I was supposed to be doing. Home was on my mind a lot, but it was Home with a capital "H," the stage upon which the Family with a capital "F" played out its inexplicable dramas. Gradually, I began to patch together an identity, based in large part on the notions I'd held onto from childhood, and earnestly set about accumulating the requisite furniture, toys, holiday decorations, and photographs to help me play my part.

I had been meeting with a group of women who believed that writing about our lives would help us stay sane, but in 1994, I felt moved to expand my horizons by taking Gerald Haslam's personal essay class at nearby Sonoma State. I remember how disoriented I felt walking among the dewy, fresh-faced populace, worried that nothing I wrote would interest anyone. But Gerry provided some essential encouragement, and when he introduced me to Len Fulton's *Small Press Review*, I discovered a universe of quirky little publications with names like *Bloated Toe*, *Hive*, and *Jigsaw*. In 1995, I marked my fortieth birthday by starting my own literary magazine in those strangely golden years at the dawn of the World Wide Web.

Like everything else in my life, *Tiny Lights: A Journal of Personal Narrative* was a learn-as-you-go enterprise, and as it grew, I did, too. From it, I learned about editing and narrative structure, marketing, websites, the importance of community, and how lucky I was to have a friend in the bulk mailing business. Publishing gave me the opportunity to work with brilliant writers and artists, many of whom became friends.

When I announced my decision to cease publishing *Tiny Lights* after nineteen years, many people likened the situation to another one of my children grown and leaving home. I, however, will always maintain that *Tiny Lights* has been more like a mother, guiding and sheltering me until I was ready to move out on my own.

Before the end of *Tiny Lights*, there was a flood of other

endings: the deaths of family members, pets, and my reproductive system. Now that my kids have left home, my parents, mother-in-law, sister-in-law, and brother are gone, and my full house is even more crammed with pieces of my childhood, it's sometimes hard to think of home in the present tense. The melancholy pull of the past is strong and sometimes threatens to engulf me. I worry that I've become incapable of appreciating life's abundant pleasures—today's sky, the taste of a ripe fig, the music of my friends' voices—until they return to me in memory years from now, freighted with meaning and accompanied by a great longing.

These days, the cure for continually looking over my shoulder involves organizing and discarding enough of the past to make room for what the future might bring. How much room the future requires is anybody's guess, but this roughly chronological accumulation of essays, with glimpses of homes I've dreamed of, longed for, found, and lost, is part of the housekeeping.

YESTERDAY MORNING, I HEARD THE OLD HEN GIVING HER triumphal cackle, a sound so rare I had to listen carefully to be sure she wasn't sending out an alarm. Sure enough, at the end of the day I found a blue egg nestled in the sawdust-filled laying box. Before I carried my prize into the house, I happened to look up and see the promise of a thumbnail moon directly overhead in the fading blue sky. My husband was due home from work, our youngest son was in the kitchen fixing dinner, and our oldest son was just driving north over the Golden Gate Bridge to visit us for the evening. I had time to lay the table and make the salad before everyone arrived. I took another look at the moon and felt the weight of the egg in my hand just before the phone rang.

I had already forgotten the moon by the time I picked up the phone, never suspecting the caller would be someone from my hometown with news of an old friend's death. By the time I put the receiver down, the sky was dark, the dinner preparations still unfinished. I realized all my stories are about loss, but if I look carefully, they all have a moon and an egg in them.

WHAT HAVE WE HERE

STARTING OUT

Home is where one starts from.—T.S. Eliot

ONE READER'S BEGINNINGS

IN THE BEGINNING, THERE WERE LAPS. MY FAVORITE WAS MY grandmother's, broad with a pillowy backrest, its warmth and scent like rising bread. I still remember her crêpey arms enfolding me, and her strong square hand with the worn-thin wedding band holding the book. Her voice as she read was low in my ear, always a little scratchy, as if she'd been praying aloud for hours instead of working silently around the house, shaping dough, stirring pots, ironing and mending. I don't know if my Dr. Seuss and Little Golden Books interested her, but she rarely refused my requests to read, and the lilt in her voice made me feel as if she, too, were fascinated by the music of words.

There is a snapshot of me in my grandmother's lap on the day I began to think of myself as a reader. I was three and not yet capable of actually decoding words, but by that December afternoon, I had asked to hear "The Night Before Christmas" so many times that as I snuggled against her, I was suddenly able to recite large swaths of the poem, timing the page turns as I remembered the adults doing. I was aware of causing enough of a commotion to bring Dad with his camera. My sense of importance expanded like a balloon as the shutter clicked. I felt very grown up and hardly noticed when my grandmother supplied a word here and there to keep the story moving. But I felt her joy and the way mine multiplied because of it. Up until then, reading had been a pleasure others could give me, but now I knew it as enjoyment I could give myself.

It would take another year or more of being read to before I learned to read anything on my own. As I began to stumble through the doings of Dick and Jane, I was shocked by how difficult real reading was and I worried that I'd never get the hang of it. Thank goodness I had laps belonging to people who encouraged me to keep trying, and whose own love of reading kept me from giving up. Even after all these years, that closeness lingers. I still feel the comfort of their nearness whenever I sit with a book.

EQUAL MEASURE

I TOOK A TRIP TO THE FUTURE IN THE SUMMER OF '62. I WAS ONLY six, so my dad drove. During the long hours sprawled in the back seat of our family's turquoise station wagon, I anticipated the wonders of the Seattle World's Fair. I was especially excited about visiting the Pavilion of the Future, which promised a clear view into the next century. I laboriously calculated how old I'd be in the year 2000. It shocked me to realize that I'd be forty-five, older than my mother sitting in the front seat, smiling and lighting my father's cigarettes, turning at regular intervals to hand me and my brother the can of Brach's bridge mix.

The thought of my beautiful mother being seventy—maybe even dead—by the time that golden era dawned was upsetting. But I took comfort in the knowledge that, even without her, life in 2000 was going to be simpler, the world of the Jetsons made manifest. She'd been telling me what the experts were saying about the way things would be, how we'd rise each morning from our climate-controlled sleeping chambers, step through the spray of electrostatic showers and into disposable clothes. We'd swallow pre-selected nutritional food pellets with our powdered drink mixes. It would be a joy to ride to work on moving sidewalks or in the safety of remote-controlled vehicles. By then, we'd know for sure if there was life on Mars. As far as I could figure, life's Big Questions would all be answered.

The proof that the new age would be calm and magnificent waited for us that summer in a city whose skyline was dominated by the Space Needle. At the Pavilion of the Future, crowds moved under the bubble-domed roof in an atmosphere of hushed triumph. It was easy to forget, as we made our way along the broad avenues of the Fair, that the Soviets were erecting missile sites in Cuba. In Seattle, in the temples to Heinz, Corning, and Xerox, the brightness of the future outshone the threat of nuclear annihilation.

But while our family gawked at the spectacle of promise— glowing dials, molded plastic, paper dresses, little space boots— my father was considering plans to build a backyard bomb shelter. A cement-lined vault appeared behind our house the summer after Kennedy's assassination. As I helped my mother arrange blankets and canned goods on its plywood bunks and shelves, I tried to imagine the evil that would force us behind the trap door that locked from the inside. A few days later, I stood on a chair in the kitchen while my grandmother pinned up the hems of my new school dresses.

I've come to learn that life is like that—there's a good chance the world as you know it will end tomorrow, but you need to pack your lunch and finish your homework anyway. The trick I'm still trying to get the hang of involves maintaining a modicum of grace in the face of fear and suffering. I know it's possible. I saw Jacqueline Kennedy shelter an entire nation as she stood with her children at her husband's funeral procession. I heard acceptance in my friend's voice just before he died of AIDS, and on some days, I hear courage in my own. In those moments it's easier to understand that light and shadow weigh the same. I must reach toward the future with outstretched hands, willing to receive them both.

GO FISH

BOBBY SCHALLIS WAS THE THORN IN OUR FOURTH GRADE teacher's side. I'm sure Mrs. McCrary would have sold him to slave traders if any had done business with Dingle Elementary School. I think back on him now and see a small, wiry, buzz-cut bundle of energy only marginally contained by a wooden school desk.

Bobby was brilliant in the dodgeball circle and on the kickball diamond, his short, swift legs pumping as he ran. In class, he did what he could to remain in motion, which, in Mrs. McCrary's rigidly constructed realm, was limited to flicking erasers and shooting off his mouth. In her never-ending quest for the silence of the grave, Mrs. McCrary was often heard to say, "Mr. Schallis, *hush!*"

I'd like to think I knew even then that Bobby was bright as well as complicated, a freedom fighter spunky enough to protest the stifling atmosphere Mrs. McCrary was so eager to maintain. But in reality, I was so intent on upholding my Good Girl status that I ignored him whenever possible. I turned in my homework on time, raised my hand and waited to be called on. I learned to handle my boredom by looking out our second floor classroom windows at the tops of the swaying sycamore trees or running my fingers along the initials gouged into the top of my Victorian-era school desk. Besides, I was a full head taller than Bobby and only had eyes for Scott Leathers, the blond, blue-eyed alpha male of the fourth grade. Not that Bobby had showed any interest in girls, except to tease them, and he'd never paid that kind of attention to me.

But at Coffee Hour in the fellowship hall of the United Methodist Church one Sunday in March, Bobby Schallis appeared before me, looking as if he'd spent the whole morning trying to worm his way out of his dark wool slacks, ironed white shirt and clip-on tie. His family was "just visiting," he told me, which explained why I hadn't seen him there before, but I still couldn't figure out why he was talking to me. At the prodding of my mother, I showed him to the table where cookies and punch were being served. It was here he asked me the last question I expected to hear from a boy who pretended to catch cooties from girls at recess: "Wanna come over to my house and play?"

Dumbfounded, I could only mumble a stunned, "I guess."

With disquieting speed, Bobby darted off among the coffee drinkers congregated on the slick linoleum to ask his parents. Moments later, he clattered back in his scuffed dress shoes, grabbed my arm, and propelled me on a search for my own mom and dad. With Bobby standing eagerly at my elbow, I was unable to communicate my deep reservations concerning his invitation, and my parents failed to heed the panic in my eyes. The next thing I knew, I was sitting on the bench seat of a Buick between Bobby and his older sister, heading off into the unknown.

Once we got to the Schallis household, Bobby's plan, such as it was, fell apart. At church, I had been a refuge of sorts, a familiar face in a sea of pious strangers, but now that he was safely home, he had no idea what to do with me. Our incompatibility was accentuated by the fact that he had been released to the comfort of a tee-shirt, jeans and tennies while I remained in my Sunday finery. Being dressed up hardly mattered to me, as I didn't go in for rugged entertainments. Coloring books and Barbies were more my line. My young swain was equipped with neither, so we shuffled from room to room in his family's tidy tract house until he offered to show me the fish pond. Cautiously, I agreed.

The oval concrete trough in the middle of the backyard was something of a wonder. The suburban landscapes of 1960s Woodland rarely featured more than a patio, a swing set or sandbox, and maybe a barbeque. This fountain, the legacy of a previous homeowner, had murky water choked with tangled plants and the look of prolonged neglect. I was about to comment on the smell of stagnant water when I noticed flashes of orange and gold among the crowding plants.

"Koi," Bobby said, marking the first time I ever heard the word. "From Japan." I'd seen big goldfish before at places like the zoo and William Land Park in Sacramento. But until that moment, I didn't know ordinary people could own something so exotic.

We quietly watched the fish going about their business,

although quiet was not a state Bobby could maintain for long. Soon, he was taking off his shoes and socks, rolling up his pants, and wading in. Ever the gentleman, he invited me to join him, but I backed away in my patent leather Mary Janes, white tights, and taffeta skirt to observe from a safe distance as he scooped up water with a peanut butter jar.

Just when I was starting to wonder how long I could maintain my expression of polite feminine interest, Bobby sloshed over and handed me the jar of dirty water. In it was a tiny, pale yellow fish, smaller than any I'd seen in the tanks at the Sprouse Reitz or Woolworth's.

"Here," he said. "A baby koi. For you."

My heart leapt, not for my brave cavalier, but for the miniature creature in the container his mother obligingly found a lid for. It was adorable in its miniature perfection, with small bright eyes and fluttery fins. I was returned home that afternoon dreaming not of the romantic overtures of Bobby Schallis, but about how big my darling koi might get.

Back at school on Monday, Bobby tried to act as if we had some sort of understanding, but I rebuffed him, figuring the best way to deal with the confusion his behavior generated was to pretend nothing had happened. The fish, symbol of love's mysterious, uncharted depths, was dead by Tuesday. Chlorinated tap water probably did it in, and the confining routine of Mrs. McCrary's classroom never allowed Bobby's tender side to resurface. I was too busy memorizing the times table and pursuing my unrequited love affair with Scott Leathers to encourage a young rebel's nascent gallantry. I never saw Bobby in church again, either.

Bobby Schallis moved away at the end of fifth grade. I'd like to think he grew up and found profitable ways to channel that boundless energy, and that he eventually linked up with a girl who enjoyed his kind of fun. But I know the people we are now are not so different from who we were as nine-year-olds. I suspect Bobby is still out there making grand gestures no one fully appreciates, while I'm busy looking off into the distance, not recognizing love when it's being handed to me.

VALENTINE

HE AND I ROAM SAN FRANCISCO'S LINCOLN PARK GOLF COURSE one February night under a round, heavy moon. The scent of decaying leaves, mown grass, and damp earth is as intoxicating as his nearness.

We race down sloping turf, stand astonished at the sight of a wooden Chinese cemetery gate looming in the middle of the fairway. No more laughter as the ghostliness of the cypress and eucalyptus give way to the Palace of the Legion of Honor, a luminous temple of stone, whiter than moonlight. Quieter still in the echoing courtyard, our warm hands explore the big toe of Rodin's lonely bronze, then pull away, chilled.

We become our own shadows, playing hide and seek among the columns. No matter how cleverly I try to conceal myself, my date seems to think as I do. He knows when I'll slip against a wall or make a break for the open. Our game is over quickly, but neither of us is disappointed. The man I will marry can find me anywhere.

THE KINGDOM OF TEACUPS

FOR MY MOTHER AND HER FRIENDS, TEACUPS HAVE ALWAYS BEEN the traditional engagement gift. When my own nuptials were announced, these loving women presented me with nearly a dozen hand-painted delicacies, packed like eggs in elegantly wrapped boxes.

At first I was somewhat puzzled by gifts that celebrated my marriage but clearly excluded my mate. These were not vessels designed for his virile grip and manly mouth. But later at the lavish bridal showers, as tea steamed in cups from their own collections, I realized these women were inducting me into the Society of Wives. I took it as a sign that one day I, too, would be expected to hold court in an exclusively feminine kingdom of linen, crystal, dainty china, and silver flatware. I found this taste of the future slightly fusty, even alarming. I joked with my unmarried girlfriends about forsaking my husband for gossip and bridge.

I didn't know much about marriage then. I couldn't know that even with a strong, fiercely protective husband, women would be the ones to save my life again and again. Over the years, I have discovered the healing powers of tea poured into fluted porcelain, how the clinking of cups against saucers strengthens a woman's laughter, works charms against despair. My mother's friends knew there are celebrations and sorrows we wives must weather. In the kingdoms we build of teacups, there is community and shelter.

MOTHER'S DAY

Perhaps I was a little oversensitive that first time around. Our bundle of joy had arrived in April, and I was still reeling from the newness of it all. Sleep deprivation and raging hormones didn't help. Silly me, I thought it was a day for awards and accolades. I was hoping for something small but expensive next to my breakfast tray.

Breakfast in bed that morning meant chewing on a bagel while nursing a restless infant. But there it was, a tiny hinged ring box, as well as something soft wrapped in tissue. With tremulous fingers and eyes brimming with sentimental tears, I tore open my gifts to discover a pair of green plastic dinosaur earrings and a T-shirt featuring a cartoon woman clutching her head and shouting, "OMIGOD! I left my baby on the bus!" Some mean, stubborn part of me hasn't forgiven him yet.

Fortunately my husband wised right up, and I think it's safe to say that from now on, he'll never try to give me a sense of humor, no matter how badly he thinks I need one.

BREAKFAST TO GO

A S THE AUGUST DAWN OPENS OVER OUR NORTHERN CALIFORNIA town, my husband and I make ready for our annual four-hundred-mile drive to his parents' house south of Los Angeles. We are loading suitcases into the station wagon at this ungodly hour because, for once, I have insisted on an early start.

We are neither of us morning people, but I grew up believing that all good road trips begin at daybreak. He grew up believing there is no such thing as a good road trip, so it's best to avoid departure as long as possible. Until now, we've been doing things his way because I wanted him to be happy. After all these years, the happy road trip still eludes him. It's time to try something different.

Following my parents' example, I instruct my husband to scoop our two young sons from the peaceful warmth of their beds into a back seat stuffed with pillows. Just as I'd hoped, the kids snuggle into their feathery nests without even opening their eyes. We hit the southbound lanes with the rising sun on our left and the setting moon on our right. With any luck, we'll have hours of quiet travel.

The rosy light flares to bright morning yellow. I join the boys in heavy-headed sleep. When I wake two hours later, we have already passed the wind machines crowding the Altamont Pass and entered the lulling landscape of the Central Valley. The traffic is light and we're making good time. We're usually just pulling out of our driveway about now. I can tell my husband would have preferred our usual plan. With a few extra hours' sleep, we could drive straight through, pausing only to hit the restrooms and refuel. Now he's ready for a break, but I can tell he's dreading that breakfast on the road I've insisted on, too.

Beyond the fitful clumps of sunflowers and jimson weed fringing Interstate 5, a cluster of gas stations, motels, and restaurants beckons. As we pull into a large lot that prohibits overnight parking, the boys rear up, baffled, from pillows heated by their fathomless dreams. I coax them out of the car with promises of pancakes.

Even before we get inside, I know the food is almost sure to be bad. Instead of big rigs, we walk past harried parents herding their toddlers with mumbled threats and half-hearted swats toward their overpacked cars. A blimp announcing FOOD appears to have crashed on the restaurant's roof. Somewhere beyond a bank of pay phones, novelty vending machines, and a weirdly stocked gift shop, a sticky table and our sullen waitress loom.

Once inside, we are lured to our doom by the scent of coffee and syrup. Even my husband smiles as his lungs fill with the intoxicating fumes of biscuits, home fries, and sausage. As soon as we're handed the huge, vinyl-clad menus, our appetites crank into overdrive.

Of course, once our orders arrive, the dream evaporates. We have driven two hundred miles for rubbery pancakes swamped with maple-flavored sugar water, colorless hash browns and eggs, and coffee made even more bitter by the film of detergent coating the cups.

But I am made surprisingly cheerful by what has disappointed the less-traveled members of my family. My parents taught me that a road trip is a series of mysteries, challenges, and traps to be navigated as carefully as any highway along the route. Those who take to the road hoping to discover a citadel of pies, meatloaf as good as Mom's, and a cooling oasis of welcome, end up, at least on occasion, eating swill from strange plates in places they pray they'll never see again. I tell my kids real travel is all about taking chances, veering from routine. This sodden weight in our guts is just part of the adventure. Bad road food confers honor on those who survive it and supplies some spice for the stories that come after.

It is now my turn to get behind the wheel, to employ my powers of luck and savvy to get us safely over the Grapevine and into the smoggy L.A. Basin. I adjust my seat, mirror, and sunglasses, check to be sure our supplies of candy and soda are within easy reach, just as they were in my childhood. I offer my family some Juicy Fruit gum, my mother's cure for boredom, carsickness, and indigestion. I think about other roads not yet travelled as I head the station wagon straight into the mirage gleaming like chrome across six lanes of Interstate.

CURRENTS

I T IS A WARM MARCH MORNING TWO WEEKS AFTER YOUR FOURTH birthday. You stand barefoot on the front porch, your new green tackle box resting on the top step, a scaled-down fishing rod balanced lightly in your grip. You squint out at the street through the glaring sunlight. You are about to perform an act you have been refining ever since you unwrapped these gifts from your grandfather. You are almost ready.

In the final examination of your equipment, you unsnarl the line at the tip of the pole, quiet the yellow casting weight that twists on the nearly invisible filament. You tilt the rod over your right shoulder and draw in a steadying breath. With your small thumb on the tension release, you exhale, flinging your arm in a long, relaxed arc. As the tear-shaped weight follows your breath up and out on its hissing trajectory, the same thing always happens. In those moments when the line flies free of the reel, the suburban houses that surround us, the power poles, sidewalks and driveways, all seem to recede, while anything green—grass, trees, shrubbery—surges into prominence, rearranging itself into wilder forms.

Once again, you have cast us into the heart of a tangled forest. Our brick porch is now a sun-warmed outcropping, and twenty-five feet away, the street becomes a wide, dark river. Its slow, straight course renders it virtually soundless, but I swear I hear a splash when your yellow weight hits its surface.

After each cast you sit and carefully, almost languidly, begin reeling in. Now the weight takes on the characteristics of a small, gently resisting fish, wriggling and tugging in staccato clicks toward the end of your pole. There's no need to rush. The catch is securely hooked. Each subsequent cast will yield similar triumph. You will catch dozens of fish like this today without ever being cruel or greedy.

I watch you through the screen door mesh and wonder. Are you merely biding your time until you find yourself dropping a baited hook into a real river? Is this morning a poor substitute for the day you can use some of the weights, lures, and bobbers you've arranged so methodically in your tackle box? I hope you are as enchanted as I am by your power to transform this little parcel of the world, but how much longer will it be before you'll want to make things happen farther and farther away from me? For now, let this manicured forest and asphalt river be wild enough for you. Take your time. There will be many other rivers in your life. Let it be enough for now to dream of the fish teeming in those dark waters.

KINDERGARTEN

HE GOES TO SCHOOL EACH DAY LIKE A PRISONER TO THE FIRING squad. No blindfold. No last cigarette. He thrusts himself across the classroom threshold without looking back. No goodbyes. Let's just get it over with. He surrenders to the solemn handshake and greeting his teacher offers each morning with no visible signs of impatience, but his gaze veers away from her kindly face as soon as is humanly possible. He breaks away and plunges stoically toward the mat where other children are already assembled. He doesn't look back. He never looks back.

Picking him up afterwards is always the same. I wait with other quietly chatting parents in front of the door he entered so grimly earlier. Other children drift nonchalantly toward the exit, pausing at the coat rack to collect a jacket or art project before deigning to greet the adults. My youngest child moves the length of the room at a controlled run, searching the faces of the assembled mothers for his rescuer. As soon as he spots me, he picks up speed and makes a running leap into my arms. He clings to me with arms and legs wrapped tight, as if he is trying to absorb me. I carry him in silence across the parking lot, choking on the question I always end up asking, "And how was school today?"

GIVE

THE SALVATION ARMY BELL RINGER HUNCHES BEHIND HIS KETTLE near the entrance to the post office, his thin red windbreaker no match for the chill December drizzle. I smile in his direction as I dash up the stairs, but once inside, I feel trapped, unable to make my way back to my car until I search my wallet for a dollar or two to push into the offering bowl. No matter how often I repeat this action in the remaining weeks until Christmas, I will walk away feeling like I haven't given enough. No matter how many cans of food or checks to charity I dole out, the gap between me and those in need seems to widen at this time of the year.

I look into the faces of my friends and see the strain of holiday preparations hollowing out their expressions. I know their faces are mirrors of my own. As mothers, we have examined our efforts in the light of some Norman Rockwell painting and found ourselves lacking once again. We are all checking our watches, calendars and bank accounts with mounting panic. Our breathing will stay cramped and shallow until the holidays finally blow by, no matter how many cookies we make, carols we sing, or gifts we buy.

There was a time when the hardest part of Christmas was simply waiting for it to happen. Waiting for Christmas is one of the greatest privileges of childhood, although I didn't see it that way then. Like my own children do now, I would let my anticipation fester into an oozing sea of impatience, and in those depths I tried to drown. I would have gladly thrown away the very hours my parents clung to in desperation.

I don't want to be a kid again during the holidays. A child's delight in the joys of the season is a wonder to behold, but an annual frenzy of expectation might prove fatal after too many repetitions. As a parent, I am freed from the burden of innocent selfishness, and enjoy the power I now possess to orchestrate some of our family's traditions and pleasures.

But I need to stop trying to shine like a star in the East for the world to follow. My children don't torture themselves worrying about their missed chances to show good will, and neither should I. I must remember that, like them, the odds are in my favor on the "Naughty or Nice?" issue. Children allow their expectations for themselves to stop at the limits of their abilities. Until the day they find themselves on the receiving end of holiday demands, most kids move through December feeling that their efforts are enough. Like the shepherds who came down from the hills one night on a moment's notice, children haven't forgotten that Christmas is a party where you come as you are.

LULLABY

THE HOUR IS ALWAYS LATE, IT SEEMS, BEFORE I CALL IT A DAY. Because I am the last one awake, it falls on me to make the rounds, secure locks, adjust windows, put out the cat, put out the lights, cover the shoulders of restless sleepers. With these small actions, sometimes grudgingly performed, I loosen my hold on the waking world and prepare to enter the realm of dreams. Last thing before bed, I often end up standing at a window in the darkened living room, looking out over our town's western slopes, somnolent under a wide strip of cloud-streaked sky.

There's never much point in star gazing. Even without a moon, the persistent glow of human habitation fades the celestial backdrop to silver and gray. Instead, I am drawn to contemplate the earthbound constellations that dot the silhouetted hillsides, each as mysterious in its own way as anything in the heavens. I wonder about the lives around each light, such anonymous glimmers at this distance, but up close, how big and bright. Once in bed, I let my eyes close over the image of these beacons, believing somehow that they will always shine, and that each one marks the place of a heart as full of dreams as mine.

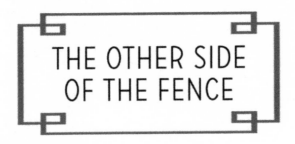

THE OTHER SIDE
OF THE FENCE

FROM THE VERY START, THE PASTURE BEYOND OUR BACK FENCE seemed as much a part of our Roosevelt-era charmer as its octagonal dining nook, curving archways, creaking floorboards, and unpredictable fuse box. We delighted in the view from our front windows, which look out over the jumbled rooftops of our small Northern California town. But the sight from the back bedrooms of that open field provided the healing antidote to too many years of hive-dwelling in San Francisco. We noted with satisfaction the violent lushness of its winter grasses, fading to silvery dryness by summer's end. Roosters began to shriek well before dawn in their ramshackle coops, but they disturbed us far less than the sirens that had broken in on our sleep during the dead hours of the city night. Enterprising moles and gophers connected their domain with ours. Possums and skunks traveled well-worn paths through our yard during their nighttime raids on our neighbors' pet food and garbage cans.

We bore these intruders from the other side of the fence no malice. Unlike the city's two-legged marauders, they were not out testing doorknobs or prying at windows. Tenacious weeds of every description migrated over our property line, but the extra yard work was a small price to pay for the pleasure of jackrabbits bounding in the morning mist and silhouettes of grazing cows and goats against the evening sky.

We never climbed over our wooden fence to ramble in the dewy grass or investigate the uncapped well and rusting farm machinery. After all, we didn't own the property, only the view. It was enough to breathe the spice of blooming mustard through our open windows and hear the footfalls of ponderous grazers as we sat in rickety lawn chairs on our patio.

With each passing year we grew more proprietary. We dreamed of a two-story addition and soaring deck like those of some of our neighbors. There would be ample privacy for afternoon sunning and life in big-windowed rooms that took advantage of the scenery. We were confident that the combined obstacles of an inordinately steep slope, overburdened sewer system, and uncertain economy would continue to secure this land for solemn cows, redwing blackbirds, and flowering weeds.

But one morning last spring the livestock disappeared, and a small tractor began grinding its way up and down the pasture. It was too early in the season for plowing firebreaks. The driver worked doggedly until the entire face of the hill was laid bare. Soon after, survey stakes sprouted in the black earth, their fluorescent orange streamers snapping festively in the wind. Men in hard hats and heavy boots arrived with the boisterous joviality of party-goers. We heard their clumsy stamping, taunting calls, and occasional grunts as they readied their equipment for the final assault on what remained of the rabbit warrens and other animal hiding places. We no longer had to set our alarm clock, because every morning at seven, the chatter of birds was drowned by shouts, snorting machinery, and beeping backup signals. The kids and I learned to stay inside when afternoon breezes swirled up clouds of dust that settled over the shrubbery and play equipment. Even with the house closed up, the boys could draw pictures with their fingers on the gritty windowsills and floors. The combination of noise and heat in the stuffy house made us all cranky. We began looking for excuses to stay away from home.

Bit by sporadic bit, sidewalks, fire hydrants, utility boxes, two streetlights, and a single curving road appeared, until finally, almost a year later, the field beyond our fence is quiet once again. The long abused earth is valiantly sending up electric green shoots, and flocks of crows huddle and peck among the tumbled clods and lot line strings. The new, as yet unnamed street, black as a river of soot, draws only a few cars up its steep grade. The occupants sometimes park and emerge timidly to gaze at the view from the windswept crest and to pause before each of the seven "For Sale" signs designed to encourage dreaming. What dreamers will arrive to buy these lots and build the houses that will someday obliterate our vista? And how long before another row of rooflines will spring up to block their view, and on and on, past the limits of vision?

Tonight, the field behind our house waits with surreal intensity, the hard, untraveled road to nowhere rich as black velvet beneath the glow of the arching streetlamps. Some evening soon the smell of damp earth will give way to the odors of barbecue smoke and newly cut lawns. The sounds of doors slamming, children laughing, excited pets, or a muffled stereo will inhabit the structures that will surely rise in another flurry of noise and dust.

Someone, in a fit of whimsy, has recently propped a life-sized plywood cow on the highest point of the hill. It stands, freshly painted black on white, looking blankly down upon the shape of things to come, a mute reminder of what life was once like on the other side of the fence.

WOUNDS

IT'S BEEN YEARS SINCE GEORGE AND I HAVE SEEN OUR OLD college friend, Les. Surprised by his voice on the phone one recent afternoon, I've invited him to dinner for the first time since his divorce. Tonight he sits at our dining room table with his new girlfriend while his children play in the next room with our two sons. Sherri listens gamely as Les, George, and I catch up, trying to leap gaps that yawn nearly a decade in some places.

Tonight, we can't resist a few favorite stories from our days at San Francisco State: "The Ghost on the Stairs," "The Mysterious Black Dog," "How Les Broke the Oven Door." We're careful not to overdo it. We know Sherri can't be all that interested in the procession of bums and partying college kids who loitered in the haunted kitchen of that old Richmond district Victorian. Besides, so many of our stories include Les' ex-wife, who always appears in a good light.

As we run through our well-worn anecdotes, I'm shocked to realize that the days of our greatest intimacy, the glorious times I thought I'd never forget, have been reduced to a fading mosaic of impressions, very few of which I can trust after twenty years. The era we spent carousing in that musty wreck of a house has become a jumble of glimpses into darkened bedrooms, the thump of feet on narrow wooden stairs, smells of mildew and pizza, imported ale and dust. We thought of ourselves as adults in that house whose thin walls reverberated with loud music and high drama, but what do those self-absorbed young people have to do with who we are now?

As if to answer that question, Les and George launch into one of their infamous postprandial discussions. This time, the men who majored in applied math are quoting statistics about new strains of superbacteria spawned from the abuse of antibiotics. Listening only to the familiar rise and fall of their voices, I feel as if I am back on the couch in that long-ago kitchen, sipping cheap Chilean red from a coffee cup, watching the eucalyptus patting its long fingers against a greasy window.

Several minutes pass as the men run the conversational ball into the ever-receding distance. I suspect that Sherri, who has been studying the tines of her fork a little too fixedly, might appreciate a detour from the relentlessly abstract. I catch Les's eye and mention that when our youngest son was in the hospital six years ago, doctors warned us that he faced less risk from his required surgery than from the staph infections raging through the wards.

I make this remark casually, assuming that Les has heard at least something of our son's premature entry into the world, the intestinal defect that had to be corrected when he was three days old, his thirteen-day stay in the UC Medical Center's intensive care nursery. The three of us can then collaborate, as we've been doing all evening, and give Sherri the highlights of yet another familiar story. But in the stunned silence following my comment, Les looks at me with open-mouthed amazement. What still feels like the biggest event in our lives our old friend knows nothing about.

George and I exchange glances in which nothing is readable. I wonder if he is angry with me for introducing the subject. I feel a growing panic at having brought it up. Suddenly, I want this part of my life to be as dim in my memory as the college days I've been wryly eulogizing. After six years, I still feel myself trembling on the edge of tears.

Although we've told our son's story many times, we've never been able to get through a synopsis in short order, burdened as we are with an excess of details. I can feel George gearing up for a blow-by-blow account that will cover the entire nine months of a pregnancy gone increasingly wrong, the anatomical details of our son's arduous surgery, his stay in the hospital, and, if I don't stop him, the allergies and respiratory ailments that have plagued our boy for years. I interrupt his narrative with a small warning cry that sounds much sharper than I intended. I do not know a signal that would tell my husband to wrap this up into one of the neatly packaged memories we've been exchanging all evening.

After all, the subject of this discussion has been wandering in and out of the dining room for the last hour or so, climbing onto my lap, whispering for dessert. Tonight, he's just a six-year-old kid who happens to have a four-inch scar across his belly. I hardly remember the baby with the IV and tubes hooked up to monitors and ventilators. At the same time, I am ashamed to be losing track of even the most horrific facts as surely as I've forgotten the faces of those college kids eating pizza around the kitchen pool table. I never thought George would be better at preserving the history of the child we could have lost.

Still, I'm relieved when we get through our recital relatively quickly. For the first time ever I have managed, in spite of the tightness in my throat, not to succumb to tears. Perhaps George and I have come a little closer to putting these experiences into a container we can open and close at will. Someday, we may have a story we're not afraid to tell.

Later, Les recounts for Sherri's benefit the time he caught his finger in a windshield wiper motor. It's another funny favorite from those days we are finding increasingly easy to forget. But tonight Les's eyes, as he holds up his scarred finger, go momentarily unfocused; his face takes on an ashen pallor. And just for an instant, even that old wound opens, the pain as sharp as memory.

CHRISTMAS DAY

In memory of Patrick R. McGriff
(1955–1991)

I GO TO PATRICK'S GRAVE WITH THE TASTE OF MY MOTHER'S Christmas toffee in my mouth. My family and I are spending the holiday with my parents, and, as usual, various plates of goodies are kept well stocked and within easy reach all over the house. As a reflex, I've picked up a piece of homemade candy along with my car keys. My sons, stupefied by Santa's recent visit, will never miss me on this unseasonably warm and sunny Christmas afternoon. This is my one chance to recover from celebratory excess before dinner preparations begin.

I drive along the empty streets of my home town. No children cavort with brand new toys on the uneven sidewalks and neat lawns. No travelers are unloading or packing up their cars. I see only glimpses of exhausted Christmas trees behind the windows of the houses I pass.

My hometown's cemetery holds none of my ancestors. Our dead are scattered in distant graveyards. Even my parents, forty-year residents of this community, have chosen to be interred, when the time comes, in the newer memorial park out near the country club. Nothing really explains why I have been making solitary journeys here ever since I was old enough to bike across town. The awkward jumble of weathered lambs and crosses and the smell of the prickly grass are as familiar to me as my elementary schoolyard.

Now, of course, my friend is here, although it still feels to me as if we've both just gotten a little too busy with our lives lately, and that any day we'll get back in touch. Not even the sight of his granite headstone has ever managed to convince me that this will never happen. Today, a miniature Christmas tree decorates the slab. Its tinsel garlands and minuscule blue ornaments wink in the slanting afternoon sun. Whoever placed this winsome symbol of eternal life did so without daring to disturb the shriveled Halloween pumpkin huddled next to it. I let the shadow of my hand and arm skim ghostlike across the chiseled stone. In spite of myself, I whisper, "Merry Christmas, Patrick," as if his Christmases hadn't ended four years ago.

Fallen olives stain the soles of my shoes purple as I walk under trees planted nearly one hundred years ago. A group of dark-haired children dressed in red velvet play Follow-the-Leader among the headstones while their mothers huddle in the family plot with their rosaries. I keep a respectful distance from two men in military uniform standing at attention near a small upright marker and the man in the red Christmas sweatshirt who paces, pauses, paces. The green metal skeleton of a funeral canopy has been erected over a sunny patch of lawn, no doubt for a ceremony tomorrow. While the rest of America is returning gifts and buying Christmas wrap half-price, there will be people gathered around a pit of new grief.

It is a busy day here at St. Joseph's. Cars full of passengers carrying poinsettias and evergreens creep down the cemetery's graveled avenues. As usual, I've brought nothing to place on my friend's grave. I loved hearing about Patrick's fortieth birthday party last year. Friends and family hid behind a mausoleum, then rushed up to his plot shouting, "Surprise!" They scattered confetti over his marker, and his nieces and nephews sang "Twinkle, Twinkle, Little Star" before they all left to have cake out of the winter wind.

Today I can't imagine my old friend being even remotely interested in anything I might bring here, no matter how much he adored my gifts when he was alive. Around me are graves decorated with wreaths, weathered toys, porcelain animals, even empty beer cans. When I try to think about what it might be like to spend Christmas at the grave of one of my own sons, my vision goes dark for a just a breath as Patrick and his new companions move a few steps closer in.

The persistent heat of the Christmas sun prompts me to unzip my jacket. I watch an inchworm hunch down the face of a nearby stone maiden, its progress slowed by the curves of her perfect mouth. A spring-like softness has made the valley air warm enough for a hatch of ladybugs. I can't imagine how these delicate creatures, whose shells match the foil-covered pots of poinsettias, will survive the inevitable freezes ahead. But on this day they swarm over the bare arms of the statues, scale the mountainous folds of their draperies, and blur on lacquered wings into the buoyant air. Small clouds of gnats whirl over rain water collected in the marble urns.

I stare at Patrick's grave wondering how a day so bright and vibrant topside is linked with the dark world below. No resident of that kingdom can be stirred by anticipation, passion, or regret on this, or any other, Christmas, or appreciate the fact that today the cemetery seems to be the liveliest spot in town. In that place, life works its busy changes in the dim consciousness of worms, the bloom of rust, in dreaming seeds and greedy roots. The clamor we lay upon its surface is absorbed and returned to us as stillness. In this way, the living and the dead continue to exchange gifts and make their celebrations.

I am lonely now for my children, their slender bones, the warm silk of their hair. I want to be back in my mother's kitchen, breaking off pieces the gingerbread man with my name on it and feeding on that sweetness. The children in red velvet have begun shouting to one another as they tightrope along the raised concrete plot borders. The noise of their merrymaking seems muffled by the silence stretching beneath our feet, but like the occupants of the cars beginning to roll down West Street on their way to holiday dinners, they carry on.

COUCH FEVER

"THAT COUCH HAS GOT TO GO," MY HUSBAND ANNOUNCED the other day. He's absolutely right. The poor old thing will never see a better day. Its velour is mangy and sun-faded. The buttons are missing on one seat cushion. The other was attacked years ago by a three-year-old with manicure scissors. I've been dying to give it the heave-ho ever since, so I jumped on his words like a hungry trout snapping at bait. I was hooked.

However, as soon as he felt the telltale tug on the line and caught that determined look in my eye, my darling tried to take it back. He got a little huffy, like I was supposed to know he'd really meant, "If a new couch appears on our doorstep in the next ten years, maybe we can get rid of this one." He didn't expect me to take him seriously. He never dreamed of actually spending money.

But now I've got couch fever, and I've got it bad. I'm wandering around the house trailing fabric swatches and staring at spots in the living room as if I could conjure a sectional out of thin air. I keep trying to drag my husband into dimly lit furniture showrooms and make him discuss armrests and skirt treatments. I want him to state color preferences. My favorite conversation starter has become, "Do you think we need a hide-a-bed?"

I'm sorry to say my husband is not handling my condition too well. He seems to think that the cure for this illness is a refusal to indulge in it, and that a purchase at this critical juncture would trigger more seizures of uncontrolled spending. Of course, that same logic won't apply when he starts looking at new cars next spring. He'll be haunting the car lots and mooning for hours over options brochures, all in the name of "research." He'll agonize over upholstery choices, and swear the car won't handle right without special alloy wheels. He won't sleep properly until something fully loaded is parked in the garage. He'd better wise up and help me get this couch. I'll find it easier to be sympathetic with his plight once I have the right place to sit.

SIGNS OF LIFE

Some summer evenings, when even leaves hold stillness, I wander the older neighborhoods on sidewalks cracked by shifting roots and earth. Years ago, before the thick branches of the walnuts crossed like fingers over wishes, I would have passed people sitting on these lovely porches or tending their gardens in the deepening twilight. Children would have been zigzagging across the streets and lawns, their shouts ribboning behind them. I would have been greeted by those who knew my name, and my presence would have added a piece to the story of their day.

These evenings, the porches no longer seem lit for welcome. They have become sentry boxes with invisible, watching eyes. No one is ever using the carefully arranged all-weather furniture. I walk past the windows of darkened parlors and dining rooms. Home life is now lived deeper, away from the street.

So I am grateful for the occasional glimpse of a dog pushing its nose under the sash of an open window, a young girl examining herself in the mirror, a man reading in a pool of amber light. Every now and then, I see a front door thrown open to discharge a group of visitors who turn and call to the others still lingering on the threshold. I sometimes hear the light clatter of silverware and conversation, or music lilting from a stereo.

It is in these moments that I have come to understand my love for others' stories. I need something to offset the sense that I am travelling in an increasingly deserted landscape. It is not enough to move through the darkness, admiring the silhouettes of rooflines against the dimming sky, to note the rise of a crescent moon. Sometimes I need to have the stories, often unfolding in silence, that are taking place in the realms behind all that wood and glass. Those stories become lamps along the path toward my ever more secretive kind.

THE ANNIVERSARY WALTZ

I WANT TO BE IN LOVE AGAIN. IT IS MY MOST EXALTED STATE. When my heart is held captive, my long, slumped spine lifts straight, my walk goes willowy. I am dazzled by my very breathing. Love sharpens my wits, but softens my tongue. I become an expert interpreter of gesture and glance. I can read secrets in my beloved's eyes, gauge the intensity of his desire as he leans close, inhaling my perfume. With love, every moment is a dance whose intricate movements I have somehow anticipated and stepped into with unstudied grace. Lately, I long to hear the music that would accompany a new passion.

I am thinking these thoughts as I walk with my husband in the coastal hills of Marin County. I have been married eleven years today to a man I love, but loving him is not the same as being in love with him. I follow behind as we walk a steep trail through live oak and manzanita. A strong breeze twirls the leaves like green lassos overheard and rushes the dry grass with the pulse of beating blood. We are alone under the violent red manzanitas thrusting huge and arterial from the spongy earth. We gawk at moss-covered oaks twisted into fetal forms. It's as if the two of us are wandering in the womb of the world. But somehow all this primordial splendor serves only to make me long for those early days of courtship, when even a ride in an elevator could feel like a deliciously feral adventure.

We climb on without speaking, and I try to imagine what this journey would have felt like eighteen years ago when we first met. I would have paced softly, almost stealthily behind him on this narrow track, feasting on the movements of his slender hands, his sure but surprisingly delicate feet. The natural beauty of the scene would have served only to magnify his glory. Everything about him would have been perfect.

Today, I notice he needs a haircut. He breaks the silence only to ask me the time. A lone butterfly appears, drifts daintily earthward and is crushed under my true love's athletic shoe. A short while later, I am temporarily blinded by a branch he has let spring back across the path. He soon picks up his pace, engrossed in the uphill challenge, forgetting me entirely as he disappears in the distant foliage. I have to shout for him to wait.

As I struggle to catch up, I observe his still-handsome profile silhouetted in the slanting afternoon light. I am disappointed to note that the sunstar, captured for an instant between his slightly parted lips, fails to engender even a prickle of response in the dark, secret places of my being. As I approach my partner in life on this windswept hillside, my primary emotion is annoyance, for now that I'm finally able to stand beside him, he is already turning to continue on.

We eventually do pause on a promontory to consider the view. "Look," he says, pointing, but for the life of me I can't figure out what he wants me to see. So much for the days when I could practically read his mind. When he moves to give me a lukewarm kiss, we falter and bump noses. I get the feeling the party's over. The orchestra has packed up and headed home.

Back in the car, we settle into our seats without touching, unable to maintain a conversation that engages either of us. It's so much easier to slip into what could be called a companionable silence and let the stereo fill in the gaps. I remember when we used to travel this same stretch of highway in his battered VW, my hand resting on his neck or knee, the music buzzing from the tinny radio speakers creating a perfect soundtrack to our romance. The songs that accompany this evening's summer sunset speak of love but remind me of all the aerobics classes I've been missing. This is music I do sit-ups and leg lifts to. Similarly, my husband heads to the gym with a Walkman tucked in his duffel bag. I suspect we have both come to value a torch song primarily for its power to stir a desire for firmer stomachs and thighs.

The romantic restaurant has misplaced our reservation. When we arrive, the only available seating is at the long counter overlooking their famous grill. As we study our menus, I feel somewhat indifferent to what's offered, for without the tender pangs of sexual appetite, I know the food, however excellent, will never enter the realm of culinary foreplay. I do not worry about my intake of garlic or the amount of daintiness required to eat my selection. Maybe the champagne we order will liven my palate and stir my libido.

As we sip from narrow flutes, I am startled to feel my husband's arm around the back of my chair. I am drawn into the warm circle of his regard. At the same time, I compare this sensation of quiet pleasure to my long-ago cravings for his touch. We don't hold our faces close as we once did, reading the secret signs of lips and eyes, but remain focused on the antics of the four men working behind the counter. Do those men like the feel of our eyes on their backs? Does our curiosity spur them on to perform more gracefully, just as I might under the watchful gaze of a new lover?

Three chefs command the grill area, whisking sauces and oils over sudden eruptions of flame. As they juggle hot pans and sharp blades in their cramped work area, they are, by necessity, rather like newly smitten lovers in their awareness of each other's movements. I think of how seldom my husband works with me in the kitchen now, in spite of his inventiveness with food and my yearnings for assistance. We no longer view such co-operative endeavors as potential romantic opportunities. Reaching for the vegetable peeler at the same moment, we are irritated rather than thrilled by the touch of the other's hand. We collide so often, so obviously in each other's way, we both feel clumsy, out-of-step.

The fourth cook, tall, blond, a bit gawky, works in isolation off to the left. He is in charge of salads and desserts, creating abstract designs with crudités and sweet sauces on chilled plates. I have rarely even glanced in his direction, but as the check arrives, he turns and looks directly into my eyes. His angular face breaks open into a radiant smile, while his arms, loaded with salad plates, open in a gesture of embrace.

I am instantly flooded with heat, helpless in the glare of this unsolicited flattery. I wonder what it would be like, just for a moment, to slide my arms around that stranger's neck and hear his whisper in my ear. Maybe the press of an unfamiliar body would force the sense of my own mystery to come back to me.

Under the influence of the fourth cook's intoxicating attention, I visit the ladies' lounge. There I am confronted by the ordinariness of my reflection in the beveled mirror. Dark circles haunt my eyes, and my hairdo and clothing seem frowsy and worse for wear after my trek in the hilly wilderness. What was I hoping to see in the glass? It will take more than the passing acknowledgement of a flirtatious man in a chef's toque to transform me.

I take a deep breath before leaving the restroom. In order to rejoin my husband, I'll have to pass that man in the tall starched hat. Will he see me and beam again? Will I trip on the carpet or collide with a hurrying waiter under his amused stare? But of course, no one pays me any mind, neither my spouse nor the fickle man behind the counter.

When I stumble up against the edge of my husband's shoe, I get his practiced hand under my elbow to steady me. I think of the times he puts gas in my car, watches the kids so I can go out, and gets up first on winter mornings to turn on the heater. His capacity for maintaining the machinery of daily existence seemed sexy to me once. I am grateful for his touch now and follow him blindly toward the exit.

The night air is surprisingly sultry as we step into the lively darkness and make our way among the weekend crowds. Afraid I'll be left behind, I grab my protector's hand, which, as usual, simply hangs from his wrist, warm but wooden. I experience the sensation of carrying an object, a medium-sized book or clutch bag. Before I release my hold, I draw his attention to the music booming from an open nightclub door, knowing he will never suggest that we go inside and dance. I make do with imagining his fingertips on the small of my back, lightly guiding me through the smoky clamor of the bar onto a crowded dance floor. We could dance to the tune we're hearing now, laughing and replaying the dance steps of our early adolescence—the Twist, Jerk, Pony, Swim. If the next number turned out to be a slow one, we could always duck out, since he has never really learned to lead and I am not sure how to follow.

I look up at the bold-faced moon, languid on a blanket of luminous clouds, and wonder what it would be like to follow a date into the fragrant park across the way. Would our kisses become the velvet of rose petals open to the night air, or would my companion and I go hard and sharp as the pair I now observe emerging from a dark side street to join the other revelers? The volume on this man's banter is turned up too loud, his cologne nearly overpowering. His date is pretty and young, but her eyes glint in the darkness. As they pass us, I watch her snake a bold hand into one of his back pockets, even as she catches the glance of another prowling man.

More likely, I would find myself re-enacting my own version of the next scene we encounter. A woman my age leans against a whitewashed wall, arms crossed, shoulders hunched. She is trying to discourage the attentions of a slightly swaying man who leans too close and breathes blurred words at her averted face. Her reluctance is clear in her downcast gaze, but moments later, she lifts her head and goes into the bar with him.

More eyes and long teeth flash predatory in the moonlight. More loutish shouts and shrieking laughter, boozy clouds of scent and smoke. I had forgotten that being in love first requires the hunt for a lover. Even the capture of a sitting duck takes place in a wilderness of uncertainty. I remember those long ago days spent half sick with impatience and fear, waiting for calls or letters that could never have come often enough. I recall being mortified by a man's indifference, or humiliated by rejection. I remember dishing out my own helpings of dismissal.

Just before we reach the car, a couple steps out of a doorway ahead of us. They have obviously survived the initial hazards of the hunt and are frolicking in the phase of love I have been fantasizing about. As they walk side by side, the air between them seems charged, like the particles found in textbook diagrams illustrating magnetic flow. The two of them are generating an energy field that holds them close in a humming intensity nearly audible to passersby.

"Should we do something tomorrow?" the young woman asks sweetly, with a smile that suggests doing nothing would be equally delicious. When her small, playful hand brushes her lover's bare forearm, he temporarily forgets how to walk. I nearly laugh out loud as she swiftly takes advantage of the pause, rising on tiptoe to taste the point of his chin as if it were an exquisite chocolate. He falls back a little, somewhat stupefied by his good fortune, then sweeps her joyously into his arms. He waltzes his pony-tailed Cinderella down the uneven sidewalk, confident that the toll of midnight will never strike.

I watch them disappear, and feel the smile lingering on my face. I imagine that wherever they go, this arduous pair is met with expressions as indulgent as mine. I think back to my tall, blond angel of the grill, and wonder if his extraordinary grin was actually intended to include my husband. Did we present a picture of intimacy that gladdened his heart, triggering his blessing? In that man's eyes, we, too, may have appeared to be dancing, not the bright, hot mambo of early courtship, but the slow sarabande of the undeniably coupled.

This possibility does not dissipate my longing for those dances of a younger time. I still yearn to be lifted out of plodding predictability into the spellbinding rhythms of desire. I already have a partner, but I wonder what music is playing in his head.

We drive home on deserted country roads, looking out at strange glowing columns of clouds, lurid in the moonlight. "*Crawling Eye* weather," my mate remarks. He mimics a few bars of soundtrack from one of the cheap horror movies we used to watch on the portable black and white TV in his apartment bedroom. I tentatively slip my fingers under the warm curls at the back of his neck, remembering a time they flowed past his shoulders. He keeps his eyes on the road, the earth maintains its steady spin, but we both know why the other is laughing.

VISION

OUR FOUR FAMILIES HAVE GATHERED AT A COUNTRY HOME IN THE tawny hills south of Sebastopol. Strawberry margaritas and good barbecue have lifted our spirits and loosened our laughs. The adults cluster around the Ping-Pong table in the garage, while our eleven children play outside in the growing darkness. The toddlers, gleefully occupied near the open rollup doors, remind some of us of where we've so recently been, while the teens give others glimpses of what is to follow as they flirt in the shadows at the end of the driveway. Under the light of two bare bulbs, we swat at blue, green, orange, and purple Ping-Pong balls, complaining good-naturedly over the absence of white ones. We settle on orange as the easiest on our aging eyes, and start popping it back and forth across the stiff lace of the net.

But the ball in this soft, shadowy light is almost impossible for me to see. With an increasingly familiar sense of despair, I add this experience to the growing list of others in which parts of the world have disappeared. I make many wild swipes into emptiness before I learn to observe the angle of my opponent's arm, the tension in her wrist, the sound of the ball making contact with the paddle. Relying on these cues, I can sometimes anticipate the place in the blur where the ball will appear, and use my failing reflexes to meet it there.

But I soon hand over my paddle for a chance at some solitude. The back deck presents a view of the nighttime sky lightened around the edges by the glow of the nearby town. Although I have factored in the brightness of the moon, the city's lights, the slow shift of my rods and cones, once again, my eyes fail me. I stand there trying to imagine the many stars that would not be invisible to my thirteen-year-old son. I can only open slowly to my faith in their existence, the glory of their remembered sparkle. I must settle for the way those distant lights silver the branches of the pine trees, glint in the movements of a cat prowling the shrubbery, add sheen to the night wind.

Lights flick on behind me in the family room. The party has moved inside. Giggles and exclamations over the homemade peach ice cream and cobbler float out the open kitchen window. I watch through the sliding glass door as the little ones gobble their fill from the ends of their mothers' spoons. My gaze moves among them as they play in a scatter of bright plastic blocks, the roomlight like the glow of candles on the altar of a darkened church. The youngest cuddles in the arms of his drowsily smiling mother. Some of the men tussle over second helpings at the counter. Everything is close enough, clear enough, moving slowly enough. In this moment, my eyes work perfectly.

HOLDING ON

Remember that in any given moment there are a thousand things
you can love.   —David Levithan

IN PASSING

I LIVE IN A HOUSE WHERE GHOSTS WANDER. AT NIGHT THEY SLIP light-footed down the narrow hall, pause silhouetted for a heartbeat in my bedroom doorway. I have stopped being frightened by the weight of an unseen companion occasionally settling into bed beside me, or the jolt of an invisible cat springing onto the covers by my feet. I now regale listeners with tales of three shy ladies in long skirts peering from a corner, or the spirit so enamored of the guy who refinished our hardwood floors it rode around in his truck for a few days. My stories never fail to elicit shudders from my audience and variations on the question, "How do you stand it?"

The truth is, I don't really know, except that I love my house in spite of the occasional disruptions. Besides, these phantoms do not occupy space needed by my family. They exist along the edges of vision, tangled among the shadows near the ceiling, rovers in that unsettled realm between wakefulness and sleep. Over the last fifteen years, guests who have reported drafts, the sensation of being watched, even apparitions, have rarely been upset by their experiences. This otherworldly element seems as much a part of our house as the breeze ringing the wind chimes in the camellia bush, or the fog that chills so many summer mornings. Only the continually shifting identities of these visitors have ever really bothered me. Because everyone's impressions remain so varied, I am led to believe no one group of spirits occupies this household. It feels more like a crowd passing through.

But we are only the third family to live in this house since its construction in 1939. No sordid tragedies have taken place under this roof. While it's true that in the 1970s one of the original owners expired in the bathtub, that hardly seems to account for the wide assortment of characters who have been inclined to put in appearances: the young woman in a neat jacket climbing the front steps, the elderly couple hovering at the foot of our bed, a huge snake twitching its way across the kitchen floor.

It is not the proper house for long-term ghosts, anyway. It is neither grand, gloomy, nor darkly isolated. All day long, the sun turns its slow clock beyond our yellow walls, delivering light at timely intervals through our many windows. The wind, funneled off the whitecaps of Bodega Bay twenty-five miles west, swirls in under the open sashes and dances in buoyant circles. Nothing can lurk here with a real cat prowling and phones ringing and boys dumping ever-bigger shoes and dirty socks in corners. For a time, an unaccountable mustiness persisted in the back bedroom, but it disappeared a few months after the arrival of our youngest son. I had the feeling my baby's colicky tantrums simply wore out hatever it was. The others only seem to be stopping by for a moment on their way to somewhere else.

These encounters have prompted me to investigate the history of the land itself. The town of Petaluma took its name from a tribe of the Coast Miwoks who occupied this area for at least ten thousand years. The current population pays little attention to the Miwoks, focusing instead on history that begins with the Spanish ranchers and mission-builders. But my friend's children have reported seeing silent, dark-haired men dressed in skins on the hill behind their house. Before roofs and trees obscured the view from what is now Wallace Court, who might have roamed the hill on which our house is situated?

I think of other places those first people walked. A few miles west is the settlement of Two Rock, named for the rock formation the tribes passed on their migrations between the Petaluma River and Bodega Bay. Our nearest cross street, Bodega Avenue, often takes me past this stone gateway, which looks like the broken-off feet of a petrified giant. I try to imagine the land before ranches and asphalt every time I drive by. Certain curves of the blacktop were determined by those who erected the barns and fences, cleared brush, and established eucalyptus, but much of our main road to the coast must have been built over a much older highway.

Oak Hill Park, which butts up against the houses on our cul-de-sac, was Petaluma's first burying ground. The city never officially annexed it, but before 1866, more than one hundred pioneers were interred there. Later, the unprotesting residents of the Oak Hill cemetery were relocated, but traces of the old graveyard remain. Friends who lived in a turn-of-the-century house bordering the park found bones in their basement. The entire northern slope retains the hushed feel of a necropolis and seems to resist anyone's efforts to turn it into something different. Some things may want to stay buried.

It seems possible that my family is living near real estate originally intended as a portal between this world and the next, a place that still carries some echo of that purpose, no matter what has been layered over it. The boundary separating us from the dead may be a membrane that can be permeated at any point, but we have heard stories of spectral portals, tunnels, bridges, fords. Just as roads often evolve from footpaths worn into the land, so, perhaps, are the pathways to heaven made. If the patterned carpets in our house have begun to show wear after only a few years of our family's wanderings, surely the feet of the dead have smoothed their own trails over time. In charts not accessible to the living, Oak Hill might be a point of departure, with our house right on the established route. When the time for the Longest Journey comes, who would not choose a well-marked way and make good use of short cuts? The sky seems closer here than in the newer cemetery on the north end of town. For those locals impatient to get on to the next piece of business, our hill might provide the best connection.

I ponder such connections whenever I visit the Bloomfield Cemetery, west of the twin boulders at Two Rock. The hill on which it perches may well have provided another vantage point for the long-vanished Miwoks and is brushed by the same winds that toss the treetops on Oak Hill. From the western edge of the graveyard, the earth falls away under a vaulted dome that seems to hold an entrance to heaven. "There's a land that's fairer than day," say some of the tombstones poking from clumps of wild grasses. It was a common enough sentiment among the Victorians, but here it's easy to picture them gazing into that dreamed-of landscape. The sea breeze creates updrafts that could lift souls like kites and set free those not tethered by a loved one's grief. Even the secretive little town tucked at the foot of the burying ground holds the stillness of the next world. I know of no recent burials here, which seems a waste of such a lovely jumping-off place. But perhaps, as in the case of Oak Hill, there are some who still take advantage of this function.

At the nearby Tomales Catholic Cemetery, behind a modern cinderblock chapel, the old graveyard opens like a book whose covers have been forced apart by the wind. While the graves themselves remain anchored to the tilting hillside, old sorrows have been blown from between the fluttering pages, like so many pressed flowers and tokens. I have stretched out on the concrete over a plot to let the sun warm my bones and to remember that no sadness lasts forever. I have run my fingers over the inscription, "All flesh is as grass," while sheep cropped the green of the adjacent pasture.

I come to places like these with my camera, peering through the viewfinder at the smooth, bare arms of statues, the folds of stone draperies, those naked marble feet. Stalking these figures for their most expressive angles, I often feel a gathering stir just beyond my range of vision, hear rustling that might not be the wind or a lizard in the weeds. "Show me," I whisper, as the shutter clicks. Nothing untoward ever slides from the shade of trees or gravestones; no extra radiance is translated onto my negatives. The barrier between worlds remains fixed, but I like to imagine those on the other side stepping a little closer, curious as to my doings. I arrive with picnics, much as people of the last century did, to keep company with my own mortality. When my eyes follow the direction of carved hands pointing skyward, I am studying a map I may one day follow home.

Perhaps that journey will require me to pass through a house not unlike the one I live in now, a place unwittingly built in the middle of an unseen thoroughfare. I may become the musty draft that rattles a cupboard in a closed room, or the dark shape darting through a doorway. And if I am not quite ready to cross the threshold into the next world, I might linger awhile, breathing in the milky perfume of a baby's blankets, trying to see how my new form fits the shape of a bed or chair. I would never think to do any harm. I might even be surprised to see terror in a resident's face if I tried to whisper some last message, forgetting, as I shed the burdens of my former life, how such visits once frightened me. I might try to tell that person not to be afraid; I am only passing through.

DANCE WITH ME

I TOLD MY HUSBAND I WANTED TO ENROLL US IN A SWING DANCE class. I had my reasons. We needed more shared activities. We needed more exercise. We needed a couple of tickets to romance. He bravely agreed to give it a try, so last Thursday night we showed up at a between-Wars era community hall with a crowd of people as clumsy and nervous as we were. The instructors were a perky and determined twosome. They demonstrated the basic principles with no-nonsense grace. As they called out commands over the big band music, we all danced together. Sort of. We may need more than six classes to work out some of the bugs.

That night after class, I woke up at 3 a.m. with the night sweats. I thought of my friend, Garnet, who confessed in her last letter that in a similar peri-menopausal moment she had entertained thoughts of me.

Garnet and I have known each other for almost a decade, but we hardly see each other anymore. A few years ago she became the pastor of a church that feels too far for a day trip, but too close to warrant an extended stay. She is not much of an emailer, and we are never near our phones at the same time, so we're relying on old-fashioned methods to keep our connection going.

In spite of her incredibly demanding schedule, which includes tending to ailing parents, a husband, and two teenage boys, along with her congregation, Garnet finds time to send me complex and delightful letters to which I do not promptly reply. A quick response would better communicate my tender regard for her, but invariably the tendency to procrastinate takes over. On the night in question, I realized I'd taken my usual loitering beyond respectable limits. I owed my friend a juicy letter to make amends for my truancy. So after changing my damp nightgown, I lay in bed cooling off and thinking about what I'd write once the kids were off to school in the morning.

I wanted to tell her about this dancing stuff, to describe the atmosphere of desperate eagerness that filled the room as thirty sweaty-palmed couples began to stumble and shuffle to the 4/4 beat. Most of us couldn't decide if it was terror or excitement keeping our feet moving, and we attempted to camouflage our confusion with wide, fixed grins. But we soon learned that no smile could save us. Those of us who brought partners were dismayed to learn that we couldn't keep them. Our instructors insisted that we would learn better in the arms of a constant stream of strangers.

There's nothing like changing partners every forty-five seconds to remind us how out of touch we're getting with each other. These days, we don't experience much close personal contact at the ATM, the fast food drive-thru window, or even the kitchen table. We think of mass transit as a traffic jam made up of hundreds of drivers in separate cars. Middle class families no longer care to imagine a home with one bathroom, one phone, one car, one television, and the kind of togetherness that hasn't been seen since the Eisenhower administration. Instead, we celebrate progress by acquiring cars, phones, social networking tools, his and her master bathroom sinks, and beds described as California kings. After colonizing these frontiers of personal space, no wonder the idea of actually getting close to someone is more than a little nerve-wracking.

But isn't a little closeness the very thing we're missing? Lately, I've found myself regretting the loss of rituals that involve cooperative effort. I don't want to go back to the time when women my age had doors opened for them and chairs slid under their rears. I don't need to be helped into a coat or a car. I don't necessarily want to go first, and I certainly want to avoid getting my cigarette lit. But there is a give-and-take in these gestures that is no longer commonplace. In them are possibilities for civility, flirtation, and grace, just like in dancing.

Most of us who take up dancing as adults have been inspired by the mysterious communication we've observed in couples who shine on the dance floor. It isn't just that they seem so sophisticated and grownup with their lips so conveniently close to the other's ear. Good dancers have to be acutely aware of their partners, and, by means of subtle, nearly invisible signals, make moving together appear effortless. It looks like mind reading to those of us whose two left feet leave us on the sidelines. Most of us believe that couples who dance together enjoy a special sweetness in their rapport. And why wouldn't they, if mutual regard is dancing's primary requirement? I wonder what life would be like if more people knew how to pay that kind of attention to one another, and what would happen if they made a habit of it.

Of course, this brings up the question of who leads and who follows. Most women I know believe themselves better equipped than their mates to set a course on the dance floor. It's hard to relax when a reluctant navigator is doing the steering. That may be one way of explaining the popularity of the dances of our increasingly distant youth. We were claiming our rights to equality and independence when we did the Twist, the Swim, or the Pony. Everyone relished the individuality and control. But our partners were forced to keep their distance as we kicked and flailed, and in the process, we might have lost track of something important.

But whether it's leading or following, dancing is about accommodation, readiness, confidence, and trust. It's all about patience and encouragement, too, and making intentions clear. It's about letting the other person know where you're going, and traveling together as comfortably as possible. Drivers who go dancing regularly might be more inclined to signal, pause, or move aside in an intricate driving situation because they know what it's like to flow harmoniously with someone on the dance floor. They might feel as anxious to make a good impression at a four-way stop as they would with an unfamiliar dance partner.

Just before I went back to sleep, I thought about how friends like Garnet help me hear the music of other relationships. When people make a point of dancing a little closer, it's easier to remember that most of us have warm hands and well-meaning natures. Once we're out there on the floor, we'll do almost anything to keep moving, not simply out of politeness, but because this may be our only chance. We are willing to lead, but grateful to follow. We just want to be noticed and asked to dance.

MOVING

IN THE CONFUSION OF LUMBER SCRAPS, HEAVED EARTH, AND ravaged lawn that has been our backyard for the last eight months, a tiny cottage has been born. All last spring I bent over blueprints, trying to imagine its future shape, feeling like a shipbuilder designing the cabin of a seaworthy craft. Throughout the golden Indian summer, men hefting tools with quiet ease hammered joists, fitted windows, skylights, pipes, and wiring. On an afternoon of impending rain, our builder made a steady dance against the sky as he nailed shingles along the roof's sturdy spine. The gutter man and stucco crew have come and gone. The carpet spreads like thick moss, the hardwood entry gleams. Now this shelter's lighted windows glow in the rain-sodden darkness that wraps our neighborhood this February evening.

This place is my new office, furnished at the moment with two camp chairs, a telephone, and an empty file cabinet. As soon as the cabinetmaker installs the long birch counter, I will begin the work of moving in.

Along with expense, risks, and decisions, each phase of

building has brought its rituals. I dropped charms into the foundation footings: gifts of stones, shells, coins, a marble from my grandfather's boyhood, two of my sons' baby teeth. I pinned photos, poems, and tokens onto the studs and plywood sheathing. I wrote the names of those who love me on the unfinished sheetrock. I have felt like some off-kilter priestess invoking the blessings of heaven and earth.

I have been moving toward this place my whole life. The questions, intentions, and desires dreamed into the structure have already made it familiar. I seem always to have known the squeeze of the brass thumb latch, the slow swing of the mahogany door, the muted fire of the carnelian walls. Tonight, I give thanks to the many hands that were guided by this sometimes faltering heart, and for the construction that began so long ago.

WHAT HAVE WE HERE

OURS WAS AN OLD YARD TO BEGIN WITH, PLANTED IN THE early '40s when the stucco house perched nearly alone at the top of our steep hill. Shortly after we moved in, someone slipped an envelope of small black-and-white snapshots under our welcome mat. They showed the house and the land around it in all its shocking newness—no mature camellias, roses, bougainvillea, or bird of paradise to soften the angles of the walls, no hedges to define the property lines, no trees and ivy to cool and shade. Over the course of forty years, it became a green tangle of interesting, if poorly arranged, plantings that I, as an unskilled new arrival, did my best to care for.

This garden provided gifts in small, isolated views—the cascade of miniature pink roses on the roof-high Cecile Brunner, the graceful droop of the pepper tree with its trailing strands of berries, the voluptuous throats of the callas, the tiny, fragrant violets. But there was no overall harmony of proportion or color, no level spot for outdoor furniture, no easy way to water or retain the earth pushing over the edges of makeshift retaining walls.

After fifteen years, I gave up trying to impose a sense of order on that which kept moving toward ramshackle and wild. What once charmed me had begun to overwhelm and horrify. Last fall, before construction began on my backyard office, I would stand on the cracked and slanting patio, or on one of the crabgrass infested terraces, and imagine a garden that could replace this awkward, work-intensive, virtually useless space. Surely, the hefty home improvement loan we secured would bring about a dream I would be capable of maintaining.

Since all of the sprinklers were broken anyway, I tried to let most of the vegetation just die, to kill off any connection I might have had for things on their way out. As the grass withered and the edges of leaves turned yellow, I kept the image of a level, green, automatically watered oasis firmly in my mind.

A year later, with still no yard renovation in sight, my charming office rests like a jewel in the palm of a penniless beggar. I watch from the window over my desk as visitors pause, momentarily disoriented by the chaos of rubble and tumbled earth. They must pick their way over wobbly stepping stones, past flower beds whose residents have foiled my plot for their demise. The survivors of my personal little holocaust lift their straggly, unloved arms out of the waist-high crabgrass, determined to endure. Their persistent growth causes me seizures of guilt, the way my children's shaggy hair, unclipped fingernails, beat-up tennis shoes, or messy bedrooms do. Every time I brush against untrimmed branches on my way to work, I think of drawers crammed with outgrown clothes; shelves that bear the weight of odd-sized table linens, fancy, unused muffin tins, forgotten toys, and baby blankets; all my smudged cabinet doors and failing appliances; those piles of unsorted laundry and mail.

There is so much to care for, plan for, do. I am at the age when every man and woman I know has entertained the impulse to walk away from the complex machinery of their lives, to turn the pages of a new book. I want to look out at a field of possibilities the way my grandparents must have gazed over the virgin prairie of Saskatchewan when, as newlyweds, they posed for a friend's camera in front of their sod house.

But there is no such thing as starting from scratch. Even in the new land, my grandparents farmed with their ancestral language, customs, and ambitions. My grandmother used no pre-mixed packages in her baking. She made bread, pies, and sometimes noodles from the staples she stored in shiny canisters in her kitchen. But she used many recipes from her girlhood and some of the same utensils for more than fifty years. I have her old potato masher, measuring cups, and mixing bowls, as well as the heavy galvanized watering can my grandfather used in his garden. They are as good as new because they were cared for with a diligence that I have never even tried to duplicate.

There is a broadness to my world, a certain casualness that my grandmother in her time and place did not cultivate. Her blue and white kitchen was tidied after every meal, no exceptions. Twice a year, she took everything out of her cupboards and washed or repaired it. I cannot possibly know the price she paid for living like this, but twice a year, she could put her hands on everything she owned, take stock, keep, or discard it.

I think of all that goes unseen and untouched in this garden, what is forgotten, what is secret. Buried in my dreams for the future is the garden as it is at this very moment. Lying hidden behind the massing weeds and unpruned branches are markers on the graves of kittens and guinea pigs, containers of leaf-scummed water, clumsy birdhouses, rusting whirligigs. There is mystery and a purpose that draws hummingbirds to the perpetual blossoms of the lemon tree. Even now, when the afternoons go cool, I seem to catch the scent of ghostly violets.

I have recently discovered a spot near my office door that can hold, not an unaffordable hot tub, but the calla lilies I dug up last year before we poured the office foundation. They have begun to wave green flags above the edges of the box I tossed them into and forgot about. I marvel at the juiciness sprouting from these warm, dry tubers, and remember the pictures I took of my youngest with his three-year-old arms full of creamy flowers, their long stems dragging the ground. There is a chunk of acanthus, too, that our friend Steve brought seventeen years ago as a housewarming gift from his own garden.

In a fit of ambition, I step hard on the edge of my shovel near a pale, spindly branch of what looks like a rose pushing through the packed soil. It must be a volunteer from a piece of root we neglected to dig out. Perhaps it is the one whose fiercely pink blooms I loved, but not enough, I thought then, to bother saving. I celebrate its possible resurrection now with a little fertilizer, pressing around its feet tiny corms of grape hyacinth or peacock orchids that I found in a shovelful of fill dirt. I edge this patch of newly reclaimed earth with pearlescent abalone shells my husband and his friends have accumulated over years of diving. I take a childlike pride in something I have made and understand a little better the pleasure I have seen on the faces of other women who have been busy in their gardens.

A few days later, I stand on what I hope will be a patio one day, cutting the dry ends from my husband's hair. I think of all the women who have performed this intimate service for their men and children, how my mother-in-law talks about pruning the boxwood and ivy as "giving it a haircut." And my mother, who, throughout my childhood, approached my unruly bangs with masking tape and manicure scissors. No one ever said, "Children grow like weeds" in my family, but I think of my own sons sprouting at every joint. As I imagine liberating a cluster of purple irises from the tangling crabgrass, I notice more silver at my husband's temples. I will feel time passing in my own body as I set that flowerbed straight, and in the stiffness of my muscles for days after.

Soon I will be digging up clumps of Bermuda root as big as my head, stooping to sort stones and bits of broken pottery, combing the dirt with gloved hands to gather more trash and treasure. I will find red plastic circles of spent ring caps, cat's-eye marbles, and rusting Matchbox cars, proof that my children once found this yard good for something. I will remember their search for Easter eggs in the wild, juicy grasses, the old bottles and glass my husband has turned up. I will rescue one of the last violets, miraculously green after a summer of no water, and move it to a shady place I cleared under the camellia.

Time in the garden forces me to reconsider my definitions of harmony and order. It is the season now for the sturdier web spinners. They have draped their glistening pennants over the fading, but still productive tomatoes, pulled yards of filament from porch pillars to listing shrubbery. Their lacy forms appear under the eaves of the open canvas umbrella or stitched across the dead heads of roses. They billow gently in the light breeze, firmly tethered to what I would like to dismiss as chaos. Butterflies and other winged insects seek blossoms that I, in a more organized frame of mind, might treat as weeds.

I must learn to be guided by the harmony of small views— the blue of bee-hummed rosemary behind a spray of pink roses, autumn's sharp-edged shadows etched on the western wall, iris tubers hunkering like crawdads in the worm-worked earth. A white butterfly rests for a moment on a lettuce leaf; heavy clusters of Meyer lemons hang among green leaves. If I put the last of the cosmos into a vase and place them on my dusty nightstand, I may be inspired to put away my carelessly tossed clothes, spend a few minutes straightening towels in the linen closet. As I wipe crumbs from the kitchen table or water the African violets before their mittened hands droop to listlessness, I am reminded that the opposite of love is not hate, but indifference. I seek out my children, then, by the sound of their voices, let my hands rest for a moment on the widening bridges of their shoulders.

There will always be too much to render radiant in my life, too many sinks to scrub and weeds to pull. Whether I work with patience or fury, everything around me seems to be in a bigger hurry than I am. My thirteen-year-old walks to school in shoes the size of his father's. The youngest wonders what it will be like to drive a car. The dishwasher breaks, the plumbing backs up, keys disappear, friends arrive, dust collects on the fading drapes. Night comes earlier than it did yesterday; the trees empty their arms of leaves. Photos yellow between the covers of albums; the garden sends its roots into the ancient hillside.

EX LIBRIS

In Memory of James R. (Bob) Gordon
(1925–1999)

FROM THE SIDEWALK, OUR NEW NEIGHBOR, A DARK-HAIRED YOUNG woman with a toddler on her hip, admires the stand of hot pink valerian taking advantage of the new automated sprinklers to flourish in our front yard. To share its sweet scent with her, I break off one of the feathery blossoms and bring it close to her face. Mother and son tilt their heads together, both noses exploring the blossom in tandem. The little one turns his eyes to mine as his hand gently closes over the pale green stem.

The three of us smile. A gift, probably the only present I will ever have occasion to give him. I am a solitary neighbor, one who is often harried and preoccupied, and these two seem to be part of the steady stream of renters moving through the house up the street. Even if he grows up here, he may never need to seek me out as other neighbor children have. Nestled in the warmth of his mother's encircling arms, he radiates the complacency of children carried by women who find this burden light and make it part of the way they balance in the world. As they walk away, I listen to his giggle mixing with the coos of a woman admiring her finest treasure.

It is by gifts that we are largely made—grand gestures, small considerations, terrible legacies. I think about the man my brother and I called Uncle Bob, not because he was a blood relation, but because we wanted the world to know he belonged to our family. He was our father's roommate at Chico State, said to be instrumental in getting our parents together. He blazed the trail to Woodland when a job in the high school art department opened up. My parents moved to town shortly after when dad joined the social studies faculty, and there they gathered a group of friends who have remained close for over forty years.

Bob told me once, a few months before he died, "You know, I've always loved you." That "always" encompasses my whole life. He must have seen me in diapers taking those inevitable first steps. I think I've have always loved the deep timbre of his voice, his luxuriantly wavy hair and neat moustache. For many years, I hoped to grow up to marry him. It is not surprising, then, that the man I did choose has a similar ear and eye for music and art, a taste for foreign food, and an appreciation of sports cars.

A bachelor, Uncle Bob often spent Christmas with us. His Yuletide gifts in particular were always lavish and impractical: hand-blown glass vases and paperweights, preserved butterflies from the Amazon, marzipan fruits, European chocolates, marionettes, and mechanical birds both satisfied and fueled an appetite for the exquisite. Each present featured elements beyond the range of my current experience, as if he were always anticipating the kind of person I was hoping to become.

The greatest gift of all, of course, is to be the one chosen to receive such treasure. As a child, I sometimes felt guilty for the greedy pleasure I took in those extravagant presents. I hoarded the candy, sets of oil pastels, bath salts, and Rigaud soap, parceling them out in private little orgies of self-indulgence. If it weren't for my mother's firm insistence, I probably never would have written him a word of thanks. I confess that the fear, real or imagined, of never tearing open another package from F.A.O. Schwarz or Gump's may have been what prompted my shows of gratitude at least a few times.

And now, a final gift from Bob, with no way to thank him: his library containing nearly a thousand books of modern art and architecture, hardbound biographies, mysteries, classics, cookbooks, contemporary fiction. It arrived, not in honor of a Christmas or graduation or wedding, but on the occasion of his death at the age of seventy-three. Nearly one hundred gilt-edged leather-bound classics now parade their solemn weight along the shelves my father made for my office. Even people who do not read for pleasure are stirred by their dark elegance. They run their fingers along the embossed spines, balance the heft of *Tom Jones* or *Aeschylus* in reverent hands, and imagine for a moment the riches that are pressed between those covers.

This man bequeathed me the opportunity to give lavishly. Many of his books have gone on to enliven the collections of friends, the Woodland Public Library, and various high school art departments. Each one exhibits his distinctive bookplate: *Ex Libris: James R. Gordon.* So marked, these books keep him a part of this world and speak volumes to those who loved him.

FEAST
OF ALL SOULS

I WAS FEELING A LITTLE DISORIENTED AFTER SPENDING THE WHOLE day in the kitchen. The last time I'd looked out the breakfast nook window, the October afternoon was in full swing, but when I stepped outside to dump the garbage, the last of the day's thin sapphire light had nearly drained from the sky. Behind the scent of wood smoke and the promise of colder nights, I could smell the edges of the crinkling leaves and the aroma of a waxing moon, musty and sharp, like the inside of a split geode. I stood on the front porch, trying to make it all register. The night smelled like something I should remember forever, but probably wouldn't, no matter how hard I tried.

I must have sighed just before I stepped into our carpeted entry, expecting my next breath to catch on the familiar odors of steamed broccoli, dust and teenaged boys. Instead, I inhaled the scent of my German grandmother's warm, clean house, where nothing ever smelled rancid or oppressive. Her cooking and baking supplied the indoor world with its own orderly weather: humid clouds from roasting meats and simmering soups gave way to the summery heat of baking *bread*, pies, and cinnamon-scented cookies. These odors gathered like the birds we counted on the telephone wire outside her kitchen window before a storm, only to disappear once the skies cleared.

On a night that nipped at the heels of Halloween, my house was experiencing some of my grandmother's weather. Suddenly, I could have been a small child bursting through my grandparents' front door, darting past the legs of uncles and aunts toward the kitchen where my grandmother stood ready to embrace me, because that night, my house smelled just like hers.

I'd just finished baking my very first batch of the envelopes of yeast dough filled with onions, meat and cabbage her German family brought to Saskatchewan from their settlement on the banks of the Volga. Thirty *berock* were lined up on cooling racks on my kitchen counters, their rounded brown backs still warm to the touch. I'd had my grandmother's recipe ever since my mother forced her to dictate the procedure, converting the measurements from handfuls and pinches to cups and teaspoons, but, until recently, I hadn't had the courage to use it. My grandmother had always supplied the family with *berock*, even after she entered her nineties, though by then, she required help from my mother and aunts. For more than two years after her death at the age of a hundred and one, no one in the family, as far as I knew, had tasted one. Perhaps, like me, they had allowed themselves to be satisfied with memories.

This year, my husband and I, bored with the tired charade of Trick or Treat, decided to invite some friends for an All Soul's Day feast. We encouraged our guests to bring potluck dishes associated with their beloved dead. At first, with my mind on the sugar skulls created for *El Día de Los Muertos*, I remembered the cheesecakes my mother served at her father's birthday every year, my grandmother's full cookie jar and the fussy cakes my friend Patrick used to make from antique cookbooks. Dessert was something I could produce without undue hassle. I'd take the easy way out and make some of my grandmother's famous, often-imitated snickerdoodles.

But then I thought of all the family gatherings consecrated by my grandmother's *berock*, how the children were given one to break open and cool on their plates while the grownups took their places at the table. I remember watching little wisps of steam rising from the moist interior while we all murmured the family prayer. Even with that bit of extra cooling, the first bites were always too hot, as if the thin, evenly browned crust contained a bit of the earth's molten core. Everyone, large and small, ate two or three or four, and after we'd gorged ourselves, there were always some left over. When I dug the recipe from my files and decided it wasn't beyond my abilities, I finally understood that my grandmother wasn't around to make them anymore.

Because I'd never paid attention to the process of sealing the edges of the dough, I called my mother to discuss some of the procedure's finer points. We spoke, then, of my grandmother's inexhaustible energy, her habit of making *berock* in batches of seventy-five or so, which meant seven pounds of flour had to be kneaded and allowed to rise three times while she prepared the filling, cleaned house and did what needed doing for whoever happened to be visiting. I remembered how, at my request, she and Mom had made more than two hundred *berock* for our wedding reception. It was hardly the kind of entrèe a bride might find in a book of perfect wedding meals, but their presence made every guest part of the family. I tried picturing all the cabbages and onions that had to be chopped and sautéed, and what neighborhood freezers stored this treasure until the Big Day. Surely I could manage a batch to feed twelve.

I shopped for cabbages and onions with memories of watching my grandmother inspect onions for soft spots, cabbage for heft, and potatoes for smooth skins and unsprouted eyes. I knew she'd approve of the sale I found on the hamburger, and while I felt a little guilty buying frozen bread dough instead of the flour and yeast to make it from scratch, I recalled how practical she was. She was known to make noodles by hand even when she was in her eighties, but she delighted in the few times I set up my noodle maker on her Formica-topped table, and we let the machine do some of the work.

Listening to the clack of the wooden rolling pin as I worked the stretchy bread dough into thin, four-inch squares, I thought of the dinnerware I would use for the party: the blue willow plates like the ones in my other grandparents' spare little kitchen, where the oilcloth-covered table was always set for the next meal and a jar of cocktail onions waited for me in the refrigerator. As soon as I decided to buy some of those little onions for the feast, I thought of the years my Uncle Phil, a colonel stationed with his family in Germany, would send my brother and me bags of rare *gummibarren* a candy never before seen in California. The feast would have to include some gummy bears, then, for Phil, now that they've so thoroughly colonized this country, and, if I could find them, some marzipan fruits in memory of Bob, a family friend who supplied my first tastes of many things elegant and strange.

With that flood of memories came others, and I spent the long afternoon in my kitchen savoring them. I wondered what was happening in my friends' houses as they prepared for this celebration, how many of their loved ones they'd bring to the party. As I slid the lumpy pockets of lightly oiled dough into the oven, I knew that my *berock* would never be as good as my grandmother's. She'd been making them for more than fifty years before I ever took my first bite. But when I came inside the house that night to finish cleaning up, I saw how the fragrance had lured my teenaged sons from behind their closed bedroom doors and into the kitchen. I gave each of them one to taste before putting the rest aside for the party, vowing that someday soon, I'd make enough to let them eat all they wanted.

LOOK-ALIKE

THE HOLIDAYS ARE ALL ABOUT TRADITION. FOR TWELVE YEARS
we'd been going to the Lucky Duck Christmas Tree Farm,
an emporium of reasonably priced, organically grown evergreens,
located on the outskirts of Petaluma. In keeping with tradition,
we'd arrive at this manicured wilderness just before dark on a day
of impending rain, and lose ourselves for forty-five minutes in the
damp shrubbery. Only then would we arbitrarily select a specimen
of the single kind available: Monterey pine.

After a few minutes of furious sawing, we'd drag our
aromatic prize back to the car and strap it on with bungee cords
that never seemed long enough. Once we got it home, our chosen
symbol of everlasting life was always lopsided, too tall, and
seemed uninterested in ever standing upright again. The fragrant
pitch made George sneeze and gave me a rash along my forearms
as I strung the lights, which always turned out to have dead bulbs
in the most conspicuous places. We'd worry about it falling over
or catching fire every time our backs were turned. We'd either
forget to water it or overfill the tree stand, ending up with a

soaked carpet. When the Lucky Duck closed its gates for good last year, we, too, were ready for a new tradition.

George and I decided to simplify our lives by going artificial. We would not be like others before us who put shining spires of aluminum on rotating pedestals in the ever-changing glow of revolving color wheels. Our tree would look natural, from a distance anyway, with branches that could be bent into attractive, life-like poses. The only thing missing, besides all the mess, would be the invigorating smell of pine.

We were convinced, especially after Karin, a friend with good taste and infamous flair, raved about the pine of PVC she brought home in three pieces from Costco. Like good parents, we discussed our decision with the children, who, like good children, rolled their eyes, shrugged, and went back to their computers until it was time to get in the car and pick one out.

I admit my courage failed me as we stood in front of the decorated display models at Target and Walmart. We had a vast array of choices—Lapland, Scotch, Manitoba, Rocky Mountain, and Canadian pines—and they all looked vague, dry, and hopelessly counterfeit. Not one of them expressed that special aura of murdered evergreen that had been such an integral part of Christmas in the past. I thought of all the outrageously priced firs seductively perfuming the air as we hurried by the outdoor lots. I pictured other green and glossy devils mocking us from the roofs of passing cars. By the time we got to our destination, the kids and I were of the mind to shun progress. Only George remained undaunted, spurred on by the vision of a holiday without sinus problems. Despite our crisis of faith, he went ahead and bought one.

And so for the first time in over a decade, my husband helped me string the lights and arrange the bead garlands in loopy festoons. After the boys hung ornaments for the requisite fifteen minutes, he and I unwrapped the rest of the gorgeous and battered mementos of Christmases past and placed them on the perfectly spaced branches. There was no fire in the grate or eggnog to sip, but one of us was actually humming holiday tunes. Somehow in the process, that arboreal imposter was transformed into a real Christmas tree, upon which dangles our family's history. Even if I don't find a pine-scented room freshener that doesn't make me gag, this plastic wonder is going to look great in the photos. Perhaps that is the true miracle of the season: no matter what you start out with, it always ends up looking like Christmas.

TURF WARS

WHEN WE BOUGHT OUR HOME, ALREADY OLD AND WELL-LOVED, the front lawn was past its prime. At first I believed I could rescue it, but after ten years of watching the weeds win, I began lobbying for new turf. I thought I was being reasonable. After all, I was the one who mowed it, watered and fertilized it, did battle with the crabgrass and spurge, all in full view of the neighbors who spent their weekends trimming their hedges with manicure scissors and buffing the leaves of their camellia bushes.

My husband accused me of being shallow and bourgeois. Why should we worry what our neighbors think? Of course, he never saw the way the downwind couple glared at our dandelions. No one asked him if we thought Bermuda grass was an endangered species that needed saving. It might be different if we were young bohemians, too poor and hip to worry about the impression our balding front lawn was making. We were, in fact, station wagon-driving suburbanites with two kids and a comfortable income. That's not what our front lawn was saying about us.

My husband put me off for a few more years by saying we couldn't afford to get the grass replaced just yet, that he'd take care of it himself someday. I had to admire his nonchalance in the face of my increasing agitation, but, for me, living with this lawn was like trying to stay serious about a man with a bad comb-over. There's only so much room in this life for pretending.

So I got real: real whiny, real demanding. Eventually, a swarm of men with pickaxes and vats of chemicals and bundles of sprinkler pipe came and laid bare the earth. After a week or so, they spread dwarf fescue sod like a green chenille bedspread over our little piece of the world.

Of course, we weren't even allowed to walk on it at first. I watched from the sidelines while three times a day for a couple of weeks the automatic sprinklers watered the lawn, the driveway, and any cars parked at our curb. Then, right on schedule, our lawn rooted.

I remember how I sat on the front porch, almost choking with anticipation as I ceremoniously removed my shoes. I'd waited a long time to experience this splendor in the grass. But as the lush blades tickled my bare feet and ankles, I realized there was something I'd been forgetting.

In the pre-sod era, I used to say that it's just as much work to mow a bad lawn as a good one. I don't know what I could have been thinking. Before I got a serious lawn, mowing used to be the work of ten minutes. The hardest part was starting up the aged Toro. Once a week, at the height of the growing season, I'd be lucky to get a bag and a half of lawn clippings. I only had to edge three times a year. The next day, as I wheeled the mower to the edge of that verdant sea, I saw that life with a real lawn was going to be different.

That first time was like mowing a swamp. Even with the mower on its highest setting, I couldn't force the machine more than four feet over the vigorous new growth before the bag filled. At this point, green magma began to spew in every direction, turning the sidewalk, my shoes, and the palms of my trembling hands the green of bad polyester golf clothes. It was like giving Medusa a buzz cut. This was not the work for unassisted mortals. I was at it for over an hour. Four days later, it was time to do it again.

This suddenly demanding lawn has taken years off my life and killed my old lawnmower. I'm already praying for the day when it will grow with a little less vigor. But if green is the color of respectability, I'm covered in it. And the best part? My husband is looking at the less spectacular yards in the neighborhood and saying, "You'd think they'd take a little more pride."

HOUSEBROKEN

Y OU'D NEVER GUESS BY LOOKING AROUND MY HOUSE THAT I
once took pride in my housekeeping. I can't tell you when
my attitude changed, exactly. It was a dream that died without a
sound—no shriek or snap—not even a whimper.

It's not that I don't remember the years of scrubbing
fingerprints off wallpaper and polishing chrome, the acrid fumes
of ammonia, the squeak of a rag on buffed glass. There were
entire decades when I shook out rugs, vacuumed draperies, and
attacked the refrigerator on a regular basis. Last week, I opened
the refrigerator and noticed a box of rock-hard baking soda
behind the jars of grey pickle relish and rancid salad dressing. I
left it there as proof of my former devotion.

There was a time when I was convinced my family would be
happier and healthier with clean sinks and regularly changed
sheets. I thought order and harmony could be taught, like reading
and multiplication tables. I figured if my mother could mold me
into the kind of adult who makes her bed and understands the
uses of various cleaning products, I could pass along this

knowledge to my own children. It's hard to believe I was that naïve.

Maybe it's a gender thing. My husband and teenaged sons outnumber me three to one. I have no daughter who might revere the family knick-knacks or appreciate the allure of flowers and gift wrap. My sons don't notice crumbs on the bread board or when we're out of napkins. They see nothing wrong with storing empty cardboard boxes in the dining room or leaving piles of clean clothes on their bedroom floors. It's possible to get them to clean something only if I articulate each step in exhausting detail and stand there watching while they fulfill the minimum requirements, not one jot more.

My husband, who can sometimes be prodded into action by feminine tears or tantrums, will, once he completes a repair, leave his tools where they fall. I can't remember the last time I was able to find a measuring tape, Phillips-head screwdriver, or some household glue, but right next to the bathroom sink is a bottle of chain lube.

As time goes by, our house is starting to resemble the exquisitely filthy bachelor digs my husband shared with other like-minded guys before we were married—with bathrooms that only got cleaned by the girlfriends in self-defense. On the occasions I have expressed horror at our domestic disarray, my men regard me with genuine astonishment.

Only a fool would fail to see that I am surrounded by my superiors in size, strength, and indifference. Now that I've learned to ignore the blobs of dried toothpaste on the counter and the way my feet stick to the kitchen floor, it's easy to pick my way around the shoes and game cartridges and extension cords. It's kind of a relief, really. I don't know what took them so long, but my family has finally trained me.

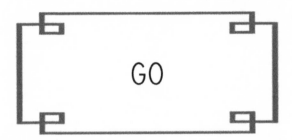

GO

I'M TELLING MY FRIEND LINDA OVER THE PHONE I FEEL DEAD inside. That little tune I've been dancing to all my life has suddenly stopped playing, and now my feet don't even want to move. She's heard stuff like this before, but she doesn't know how desperate I'm feeling this time. I picture her cradling the receiver on her shoulder, closing her eyes against the fumes of the onions she's chopping for dinner. Her still-beautiful throat has that slightly rope-burned look women get after forty—like we've all survived a hanging. She murmurs something from our litany of reassurances and then it's time to hang up because my kitchen is suddenly full of fourteen-year-old boys.

"Mom," one of them says, "do we have enough dinner for these guys?" He jerks his thumb to indicate three others who are acting like pieces of time-lapse photography, legs lengthening, chests expanding, upper lips sprouting hair right there on my linoleum. And before I know it, I'm grilling extra chicken and making macaroni and cheese and feeding this maelstrom of mouths. Then they're jostling each other hard on the way to the bathroom for that extra deodorant, hair gel, and mouthwash.

Now I'm driving to the bowling alley in a station wagon that doesn't have enough air in it, and the radio's as loud as their laughter. I get panicked thinking that it won't be long before there won't be an adult driving them anywhere on a warm Friday evening in spring, heading for a place packed with girls.

The bowling alley is overflowing with girls clustered like pins just waiting to be knocked down. The chatter spilling from their candy-scented mouths is deafening. I watch my son climb into a loose and easy stance, hands in the pockets of his baggy pants. He is waiting for me to leave. He steps aside to make room for a blonde who crests like a wave against his best friend's chest. I see that the bowling alley, the parking lot, the whole world, belongs to them, which makes me glad, in a way, because I am too tired to know what to do with it.

I'm back in the car, and the radio's just as loud as it was a few minutes ago, but there's something about the music, even though it belongs to them, that brings a little sway to my hips. My oldest son's having fun, has a couple decades, maybe, before he finds himself wondering who he is anymore. My other boy, the eleven-year-old who still sits in my lap when he's sad, is waiting to be picked up at a house out in the country, where he's been sliding down grassy slopes and listening to the nattering of his friend's goats. I'm heading west and smiling a little, because in spite of everything, my body is still seeking the beat on the stereo. I've got my foot on the brake at a red light. When the signal changes, I see that the evening sky behind it is tinged with that same green, like everything in the world is saying, "Go."

TIME TRAVELS

Last night, I woke at 2 a.m. to the sound of quiet feet in the dark kitchen. It turned out to be one of our hungry sons, just as my logical mind suspected, but not before my wilder mind imagined some sinister intruder. I commiserated with Dante about the noisy floorboards, then checked the locks before going back to bed.

An hour later, I was roused by a small riot outside our bedroom window. I listened as a neighbor's toddler cried, a dog barked, and something large and ponderous rummaged in the ivy. My husband experienced a different night altogether, sound asleep beside me.

Time for each of us is ours alone, even as we flow with all creation in the wider, deeper river of it. Time may not be a river at all, but as I make my groggy way into a new morning, that's the way I think of it. Isn't everything designed to travel on currents, on chartable paths of water or wind? Even those who rustle in the weeds or set floorboards creaking in the middle of the night are creating ripples in the wake of their passage.

As we ride the currents of this vast, mysterious life, time gives us everything we know about the world. The hard shocks, the restless nights, and the slow unfolding of wisdom are ours to keep, to make of what we will. Only the Rip Van Winkles of the world remain unchanged by the journey, and even they must wake sometime.

Tomorrow, I am likely to forget all about sitting here at my desk with the morning sun illuminating the pages of an opened ledger, the *tock-tock* of my office clock, the sights and shadows outside my window. This brief but welcome peace may slip into irretrievable depths unless I mark it in some way, perhaps by writing about it.

When all is said and done, this morning may not hold much in the way of deep significance for me, but somewhere, not very far away, someone is reading a letter, answering the phone, or staring at the ruin of an unmade bed as the course of her entire life changes. I am not sure how I feel about living in a world where anything is possible. I only know that time gives us the gift of our selves as we each live out our different stories.

GLORY

THE RACQUETBALL COURT IS ALWAYS STUFFY ON TUESDAY nights. Smells of floor wax and old sweat assault me as I push open the court's windowless door, late as usual. The other five have already arrived with the net and what looks like a blue, slightly softer version of a volleyball. We're here to play a hybrid of racquetball and volleyball, a game with an embarrassing name: wallyball.

We slightly awkward middle-aged parents glance shyly at one another, like seventh graders reporting for gym in our big, stiff shoes. Then someone begins bouncing the royal blue ball smartly against the hardwood floor or boosting it into the air. This is the signal for Tim and Joseph, the only men, to take positions on opposite sides of the net. Leane, Sandy, Mary and I find our places after a delicate exchange of glances and small talk that factors skill levels and whose turn it is to play with whom.

Soon the ball is arcing over the net and angling off the walls, its syncopated drumbeat stilling our chatter, drawing us, one by one, into an awareness of being alive together. Uncooperative bodies that were lurching and hesitant just moments before gather grace and energy. Suddenly, we aren't tired anymore. We discover that when we relax, time expands. As we crouch and pass and leap to the sound of the ball smacking against the walls, our palms, and forearms, a state of exultation gradually overtakes us.

This weekly dose of glory is not the result of my athletic prowess. As a kid, I did what I could to avoid sports. I hated the scrutiny of crowds, the bite of competitive play, my gut-knotting fear of letting teammates down. I had to turn forty before I could admit that I might have been missing something. At our athletic club, which caters to racquet sports I am too intimidated to consider, I heard about a group of people who'd been playing wallyball every week for ten years. I couldn't imagine how a sport with a name like that could be so compelling, but the word "fun" kept cropping up as people tried to describe it. Since fun was something I'd never associated with team sports, I got curious enough to convince a group of friends to try it.

I found little to rejoice in during our first games. A corrective comment or disapproving look from a teammate could virtually blind me, set the choke of tears strangling my throat. With every muffed play, I relived the despair of the skinny kid who was always among the last chosen for any team, the one who was lucky to get a "C" in P.E. To cover my mortification, I resorted to my lifelong practice of making fun of myself. I still felt like the girl who cried every time she fell down, even when she wasn't hurt. But I persisted, knowing this might be my last chance to play on a team that would have me. After many weeks, I finally began to notice that I wasn't the only one making mistakes. Once I stopped worrying so much about looking foolish, my game improved. Suddenly, it felt good to laugh at myself.

I'm not the only player learning to abandon herself to pleasure. After four years and hundreds of games, the women in our group still apologize whenever we miss a shot. Even the men are awkward when we high-five, razz each other and gloat. But appreciative hoots or roars of outrage echoing off the court's high ceiling prompt us to unleash our confidence, attempt some cockiness. We form fierce alliances with teammates, who, in the next set, might try to stare us down from the other side of the net. We've become accustomed to the sting of the ball bounced off our noses, to see a blackened or swollen finger as an insignificant injury. We shout a lot and display our bruises proudly. We grin at each other when we begin to sweat and know we've played well when we ache afterward. The more damp and flushed we become, the more beautiful we are to one another.

But no matter how mightily I cultivate my newfound sportsmanship, I may never again experience the splendor of truly aimless play. Not having been particularly spontaneous as a kid, I have become one of those adults who has to schedule my fun, who wouldn't play at all if it weren't so good for me. What's worse, I find myself preaching the benefits of exercise to others, especially my oldest son, a long-legged, dreamy sixteen-year-old who sees no use for vigorous physical activity. Although his thirteen-year-old brother is showing similar tendencies, I don't fret about him so much. That one was born knowing how to ride a surfboard and creep like a ninja out of enemy range during squirt gun wars. He even joins me occasionally on the wallyball court. But the oldest considers walking three blocks to the 7-11 for a Slurpee an adequate dose of exertion in a day spent on the phone, TV, and computer.

When the kids were younger, their father and I weren't too surprised by their seemingly inbred distaste for organized sports. Soured as our own childhoods were by paralyzing self-consciousness or abusive coaching, we may have inadvertently encouraged it. We figured the dullness of their competitive edge was genetic, and vowed never to pressure them into signing up for soccer or baseball. We knew they didn't need football to make men out of them.

We have always been reasonably health-minded, however, so we tried to promote the solitary joys of roller-skating, skateboarding, bike riding, and boogie boarding, all of which require a certain amount of equipment. Our garage has become a warehouse of outgrown bikes, wetsuits, helmets, and roller blades, all in mint condition. My husband is famous for outfitting other people's children and taking them on mountain biking or boogie boarding expeditions. When I contemplate my offspring's utter lack of enthusiasm for such adventures, I've wondered if they'll ever know what they're missing.

Granted, a troubling memory persists of my mother standing in the doorway of my bedroom when I was about ten and sputtering, "But it's such a beautiful day! At least go read *outside*!" I prefer to remember myself as a six-year-old in ballet slippers dancing like a dervish to show tunes blaring on the living room hi-fi. I think of the hours spent circling our block with metal skates clamped to my Keds, or crisscrossing town on my Schwinn

3-speed, nonchalantly, no hands. These days, ways of reaching, twisting, and balancing that I'd thought I'd forgotten return to anchor me in my body, whether I'm walking along a grocery aisle or making a lunge for the wallyball. I'm even grateful for the ways long-ago injuries shape my present movements with twinges that remind me to breathe and be careful.

The body never forgets. My husband, after an adolescence spent surfing, moves through crowds as if he were entering shorebreak, shoulders back, arms slightly away from his sides, prepared for the shock of cold, the tug of currents. Another man I know still maintains the loose-limbed amble of a pitcher approaching the mound. Sometimes in conversation, his big-knuckled hand will arrange itself around an invisible baseball. A former dancer sits upright in her chair, folding like a fan to retie her shoe. I want my son's body infused with such history, one that will repeat itself in odd moments of grace.

And yet, what do I really know about my oldest boy as he moves toward a manhood beyond my range of vision? He's always lived on a steep hill in a neighborhood with no boys his age. No impromptu games of baseball in the twilight, no safe place to skate alone or practice riding a bike. Until he started junior high, I arranged his play the way I now schedule my wallyball sessions. He grew up with friends whose parents sunscreened, helmeted, and guarded them relentlessly throughout their childhoods. Is it possible to develop a passion for a sport, or anything, for that matter, if someone is always supervising?

Lately I've noticed, as he chops an onion in the kitchen or grips the steering wheel of the family station wagon, how the tendons in his hands and forearms have been sculpted from playing the electric bass. When I watch him stylishly vault an accidentally locked gate at his grandparents' house, I realize that he's put in time climbing trees and building forts. He may stroll around town with the gait of a sleepy giraffe, but I remember how, at the beach last summer, I goaded him into running with me along the sand. We trotted side by side, his breath coming with an almost irritating ease. Partly as a joke, partly out of self-righteousness, I began to race him. Soon, the harsh pleasure of salt air in my lungs and the pounding of my bare feet on the shore obliterated my desire to prove some point. We ran together companionably for a few minutes. Then, the boy who'd been complaining about being forced off his beach towel grinned and burst ahead, his long pale legs unspooling a distance between us. The farther away he got, the more clearly I could see the way his glory lit the air around him.

DRIVER'S ED

M Y SON WILL BE GETTING HIS DRIVER'S LICENSE SOON. Consider yourself warned. Come summer, it might not be a mom with thirty years of experience behind the wheel of that blue station wagon. Instead, you may be encountering someone with, shall we say, more youthful attitudes and responses.

I confess I'm a little worried. My son has so much to learn, and Driver's Ed wasn't much help. What kind of antiquated nonsense are they teaching these kids anyway? After finishing the course, he's still under the impression that a car is a potentially dangerous weapon. He remains acutely aware of the laws of physics and buckles up every time. In spite of what he sees every day, he thinks tailgating is bad form, as is failure to yield right of way. Unlike more experienced drivers, he takes stop signs seriously and looks both ways before pulling into traffic. He even uses turn signals. He'll drive you crazy if you end up behind him, because he hasn't figured out how to add at least seven miles an hour to any posted speed limit His dad and I have been doing our best to set a modern example, as have so many of you. But we're having a tough time convincing him that only losers follow the rules.

Fortunately, my son is a smart one. He'll catch on to the way things really work. He'll start rolling through stop signs and shrouding his lane changes in mystery. He'll learn to drive half-asleep or staring into the rearview mirror and using his phone. Before you know it, he'll be out there speeding, hugging your blind spot, cutting you off, and communicating with his middle finger like a veteran.

In the meantime, I am hoping you can give him a little distance and remember what driving was like before you got the hang of it. It's really true that you're only young once. Your understanding could help keep my son alive until he learns to drive like the rest of us.

LOST

I'VE JUST HAD A LESSON IN MORTALITY. MY COMPUTER'S HARD drive died.

"What happened?" everyone asks, and I tell them it's a mystery. The machine performed without a hitch until July 1. Then everything, including the upcoming issue of *Tiny Lights*, became invisible—part of a "failure to boot."

The men in my household sprang into action. My son installed a new hard drive, along with a second drive for daily backup. My husband shipped the tiny corpse to a place called Drive Service for autopsy and data recovery. I responded to the situation by attacking weeds and various overdue household projects. By the time I'd finished painting the bathroom, Mark from Drive Service called to say he was sorry, but the hard disk itself had been corrupted. He could only retrieve my email files. The rest, he said, is history.

Weeks later, I approach my computer warily, sniffing for the acrid scent of disaster. There is no evidence of fire, theft, or flood. Nothing about the office appears out of the ordinary. No one else seems to notice how empty the room feels with three years' worth of writing missing.

But what if there had really been a fire or flood or vandalism? I remember spending one rainy winter afternoon with a woman whose home had just burned to the ground. A few of us hunkered at the site of the tragedy, poking through the charred rubble. We uncovered only burnt corners of photos, twisted bits of jewelry and silverware, a few ruined books, tapes, and journals. Nothing seemed worth saving. We lay the remains of her earthly possessions at her feet as she stood whispering, "I just want to walk away from it all, just walk away."

I'm one of those people who can only walk a beam if it's less than two feet off the ground. Raise the bar any higher, and my courage and sense of balance fail. I look around my office at shelves crowded with memorabilia and books. On the floor are file boxes of old letters, news clippings, magazine articles, and back issues of *Tiny Lights*. I can run my fingers down the uneven spines of eighty-three journals and notebooks. I still mourn the contents of my computer, but the presence of these accumulated words steadies me, gives me the impression that I have something to fall back on, a lifeline, a safety net. I tell myself I'm as safe as I ever was. Time to step out again. As my friend Tony said, tapping his finger lightly against his skull, "A least *your* hard drive wasn't erased. You haven't really lost anything."

Note: Shortly after I finished this piece, Mark from Drive Service, thanks in large part to my husband's relentless pleading, tried one more thing three more times and found all the missing data. It's another story now—or is it?

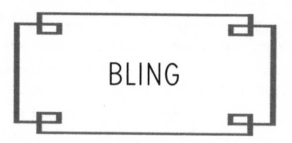

BLING

I ADMIT IT, I'M SHALLOW. I'M SHALLOW AND GROWING MORE SO BY the minute. Maybe as I'm getting older my juices are drying up and the pebbly bottom of my soul is that much closer to the surface. I don't know. But until a few years ago, I never thought I'd be so excited about a piece of jewelry, let alone a diamond ring.

Just because I pressured my husband into buying this ring is no reason to think it doesn't really qualify as a gift. Maybe you haven't been married long enough. I confess in years past I was shallow enough to have dreamed of a prince who would get down on bended knee with a proposal or a pendant. I longed for the kind of husband who would surprise me with a new Mercedes topped with a giant bow. That was before I married a guy who will thrust an armload of flowers at me while I'm sitting on the toilet or give me flannel pajamas for Valentine's Day. For nearly a quarter of a century, my mate has channeled his passion into practical gestures, proving his love by making sure the bills are paid, my computer is debugged, and my tires are rotated.

Therefore, his willingness, after only three reminders, to take me to a nice jewelry store seemed awfully romantic.

His compliance in this matter surprised me almost as much as my urge for a flashy ring. At the time we got engaged, I thought diamonds and ivory were about on par—symbols of suffering and subjugation. The idea of sporting a big rock revolted me, although I'm sure I wouldn't have refused one if he had insisted. We settled on a dainty sapphire, my birthstone. I wore it shyly and proudly during the wedding preparations, and happily enough for a few years, until the stone fell out. I didn't think much about it for a long time after.

But marriage in the long haul, is all about accumulation—children, property, satisfactions, and disappointments. One day last autumn, I noticed that the contents of my jewelry box did not reflect my husband's years of devotion to his beloved and now middle-aged wife. Instead, it conjured the image of a woman whose wardrobe comes from Walmart and Ross Dress for Less. It was the unremarkable spoils of someone who, in her salad days, had neglected to engage in some long-range investment strategies.

As I pawed over my motley assortment of hippie pendants and confirmation crosses, I found myself pining for something deeply lovely, a flashy gem that would spark a little covetousness in another woman's soul. I had given this man my youth, and what did I have to show for it? I didn't want anything too ostentatious to call attention to my liver spots and wrinkly knuckles, but I still felt the rocks of desire scraping along the bottom of my little boat.

The birth of this yearning helped me understand why my husband sometimes finds me confusing. But it also seemed like a good time to tell him what I wanted, even if I couldn't explain why. With Christmas coming and another quarter of a century of marriage looming, what better time to start communicating?

So on a bleak December Sunday, he took me to the same jewelry store where we found our wedding rings twenty-four years earlier. This time, I had the sense to accept the idea of one-stop shopping. He waited patiently, even as his back began to twinge, while I waded through the gemstone cases. I tried on topazes, garnets, and more sapphires. They were all lovely, but nothing called to my shallow soul, until the sales clerk suggested we take a peek at the diamonds.

At first, I thought I was impervious to tradition's clichè. I found myself swerving from the freakishly expensive stones—I didn't think I could love something that much—but the sight of a slim rose gold band set with fifteen tiny diamonds took my breath away. Suddenly, I was filled with diamond lust. Fortunately, my man has learned to read the really important parts of my mind, so we could pretend I had nothing to do with the final purchase.

The store had to order a ring in my size, and in the waiting, those diamonds glittered in my mind's eye like the contents of Aladdin's cave. I imagined the dazzling effect this ring would have on those who encountered me. I would be recognized as a woman of substance, a being worthy of jewels in spite of her shallowness. I even fantasized about the moment of presentation, conjuring the taste of champagne and the sounds of gypsy violins.

When my husband finally brought the ring home in its fancy velvet box, he handed it to me while I was putting away laundry. I told him he could do better than that. He stared at me uncomprehendingly for a few moments before he took back the box, removed the ring, and nearly dislocated my knuckle trying to put it on my finger. I stopped him before any real pain ensued, laughed, and slipped it on myself. I closed my eyes and kissed him like a woman who has just been given the world, while in my shallow soul I conjured dreams of the next time the need for diamonds might strike again.

GOING ALONE

... now and then an angel, in a kind of marvelous transport, as if unable to restrain his bliss, suddenly, for a single instant, unfurled his winged beauty, and it was like a burst of sunlight, like the sparkling of millions of eyes.

—Vladimir Nabokov, The Word

IT IS LATE SPRING AND THE CIRCUS HAS COME TO TOWN. LIKE THE flocks of migratory birds that visit our marshes on their annual travels, this band of clowns, acrobats, and jugglers arrives at the local fairgrounds around the same time every year. I have learned to watch for them. This afternoon, as the sun edges into a fogbank blowing in from the west, I follow parents herding their children toward a white vinyl tent pitched on the prickly grass. Passing a cranky three-year-old dragging on his mother's wrist, I'm glad those years are behind me. My husband and teenaged sons can help themselves to the stew I left on the stove if they want dinner before I get home.

In the four years I've attended this circus, I've always come alone. I'm accustomed to the ticket seller asking me to repeat my order when I request just one admission. The ushers look behind me for youngsters who might be dawdling. My parents raised me on a steady diet of parades, carnivals, and roadside attractions, and I expected my own offspring to find magic in county fairs and Broadway shows. Instead, they inherited their father's distrust of crowds. The last time I dragged our sons to a live performance, the youngest, then fourteen, leaned over and hissed, "Mom, you're clapping too loud."

Alone in broad daylight, I don't have to explain myself to anybody. And once inside the tent, there's always enough company. The ushers sandwich me among other families on the main aisle, where vendors hawk refreshments, balloons, and light-up toys, and passing toddlers use my knees for balance. In the past, mothers with children have welcomed me with an occasional smile or comment. This year, however, two silent, broad-shouldered men who do not extend their attentions beyond the youngsters tucked next to them barricade me on both sides.

Today, the big top, such as it is, is not even half full for the afternoon performance. I've never been bothered by a low turnout before, but the men beside me are peering around us at the unoccupied seats as if looking for evidence of charlatans or thieves. No happy buzz of anticipation stirs the air. Instead, children still bleary-eyed from naps poke each other or pester their parents for cotton candy. In the row behind me, a mother threatens, "You really want something to cry about?" Luckily, before she makes good on her offer, the tinsel curtain parts, and a ringmaster garbed in shabby polyester takes the spotlight.

Past productions have made do without this relic of circuses past, but here he stands in black vinyl boots and top hat, resurrecting clichès like "astounding" and "death-defying," between ear-splitting bursts of microphone feedback. He seems to be promising an old-fashioned storybook circus with calliope, clowns, and sprightly acrobats. Then, music reminiscent of TV's "Survivor" crackles through the single speaker. This circus is having an identity crisis.

For the first time, I notice how many members of this troupe, founded by a family from the Yucatàn, share not only the same last name but an obvious resemblance to one another. As the cast tramps out for the opening parade number, I am shocked by how short and unprepossessing they appear. The women, in particular, seem lacking in glamour. Even in their clinging, sequin-trimmed costumes and feathered headdresses, they look like a tribe of housewives, not athletes. They are firmly packed, squat, unremarkable, with plump arms and calves, not half as impressive as the women whittled down to muscle and sinew who command the spotlight at my gym.

The performers straggle off, leaving behind a heavily eye-shadowed young man billed as the Hula Hoop Hero. He bats his mascara-laden lashes and begins spinning multi-hued rings on various parts of his body. He is graceful, skilled, and incapable of charming anyone, even someone like me, who, under normal circumstances, is moved to tears by amateur talent shows and junior high school marching bands. I have fallen under the spell of this sullen crowd, and even after the doomed youth walks on his hands with hoops whirling around his neck, ankles and thighs, I slouch in my seat like one of my own teenagers. I let the guarded applause of the others determine the volume of my own. To the Hula Hoop Hero's credit, he carries on, a smiling, perspiring sacrifice. His final bow is elegant, almost defiant.

Thankfully, the acts that follow become more difficult to dismiss. The circus men are especially brave, and my heart opens at the sight of them risking injury for the chance to walk a tightrope juggling fire or chase each other on motorcycles inside a cage called the Globe of Death. To my relief, my more vigorous clapping now blends with the response around me, but I remember years when the crowd whooped and shrieked during similar feats. Our reticence must be disappointing.

One flamboyant young prince taunts us for more applause as he cavorts twenty feet above our heads on a contraption that looks like a cross between a giant hamster wheel and a log rolling end over end. He works without a net, and the one time he stumbles, I gasp at the thought of him falling. This tiny sound causes the men beside me to swivel their heads and briefly regard me like fairgoers watching the roller coaster but refusing to ride on it.

The circus men may court admiration, but the circus women are another story. Perhaps they are saving their energies for tonight's crowd, but this afternoon, they act as if we bore them. Shrugging off their earthbound heaviness, they vault onto the shoulders of their husbands and cousins, perform handstands on the palms of their fathers, all the while actively ignoring us. Their muscles hardly ripple as they wind themselves with detached languor on ropes suspended from the roof of the tent, or balance on their bellies on hanging bars, backs arched like strung bows. They deliver themselves to their men, not as daughters or lovers, but as Indian clubs or juggling balls. These women test the limits of their bodies like domestics who do the work of the world with no hope of recognition. There seems nothing we can do to relieve them of their drudgery.

A clown approaches the barrier that's been separating the audience from the circus. This is no Bozo or Ronald McDonald, bouncy and jovial with a gash of red where his smile should be. This is a thoughtful clown, neatly dressed, ironic, Russian, whose every gesture seems to ask who the real fool is. That is why even his juggling makes the crowd nervous. He has a plan and is going to make use of us.

There is nothing menacing about the clown's manner, but when he steps over the low stage wall into the audience, I hear a startled yelp, followed by a flurry of laughter.

Nothing else breaks the silence as the clown's dark eyes search the crowd. I have left my gaze unguarded, assuming I am too far away to be noticed, but then, from more than fifteen feet away, his eyes find mine. Who is this clown with the power to see into me and how is it possible that I am able to do the same with him? For a moment, we stare, oddly at peace, drinking in the other's aloneness. But when he begins to head in my direction, brushing past a woman in the second row and her brood of suddenly silent eight-year-olds, I am stricken, like an animal in oncoming headlights. The closer he gets, the more I want to hide behind the stiff, warm wall of the man to my left, even if he has no interest in shielding me. In desperation, I shut my eyes, the better to shrink inside, like I did as a child when nightmares hunted me in my bed.

The clown's shadow blankets me like fog, and when I open my eyes, I am looking at the place where his neck emerges from his striped knit shirt. I watch, fascinated, as his bare hand reaches out, not for me, but to the man on my left, who extends his own hand as if hypnotized. Their fingers meet to shake hands inches from my face. I am that close to being chosen.

The clown leans close and murmurs, "Come, sir, we will have some fun," in a heavy Russian accent. To my utter amazement, the man, having thus far resisted every invitation to participate, suddenly surrenders. He stands and follows blindly into the ring, knees jerking like a marionette's. Once in the spotlight, he obeys every command, swiftly growing more animated, inventive even, as he completes a series of silly tasks.

The audience is buoyed by this display of courage from one of its own. We laugh and bestow on him some of our most appreciative applause, even when his antics involve nothing more complicated than tossing popcorn at the clown's open mouth or acting as a holder for a toilet paper roll.

By now, I envy my neighbor's opportunity to abandon his inhibitions and join the circus, but his show business career brings no lasting transformation. As he takes his bow, I expect him to carry traces of his boyish gaiety back to his wife and children, but once he steps back into the audience, his gait and features stiffen. By the time he returns to his seat beside me, the boy inside is wood again.

Other acts whirl by in a blur—juggling, acrobatics, feats of quick-change artistry—but no matter what spectacle is unfolding in the ring, I feel as if we are under a spell no one is capable of breaking. There is no one to rescue us from the just-missed quality of this experience, certainly not the ringmaster, whose only other function has been to urge us to stock up on concessions at intermission. The performers have given what they can or what they must, but as the music builds for the Big Finish, children fidget and adults rub their necks or check their watches.

Four men stride into the spotlight dressed in purple and gold spandex. They clamber on rope ladders up where the tent roof holds back the sky. They look down on us and nod, calmly adjusting the trapeze rigging. From their high perches, our upturned faces must appear riddled with dark holes, while from below, we see only the lines of their muscled sleekness.

At some secretly exchanged signal, the catcher, alone on his platform, claps his hands once, sharply, releasing a small cloud of talc dust. He swings onto the trapeze and soon, he is swaying by his knees, ready to receive his brothers.

The chosen one on the opposite perch grabs an empty bar and leaps toward him, riding the arc to its farthest edge before letting go and falling. The outcome is predictable, but the moment the catcher plucks this man out of the air by his wrists, the aerialists begin to play, not to the audience, but to each other. In this final volley of somersaulting leaps and catches, they grin at their own madness and shout in celebration of it. Intoxicated by their daring, they stop listening for our applause. Once they forget us, they are like birds that have no need to concern themselves with the ground. And until they end their flight by plunging headlong into the waiting net, I am finally free to join them.

When the house lights go up, I see that I must pick my way over the litter of popcorn, plastic cups, and peanut hulls left by my fellow circus-goers. It seems that even with magic, there's always a mess to clean up. Three of the aerialists are standing near the exit, arms easy across one another's shoulders, eyes still lit with triumph. I pass them tongue-tied, too shy to offer praise, but I see them smile at a small boy who leans toward them from his father's arms and promises, "Someday I'm going do that, too!"

It's time for me to leave this family and return to my own. I still have time to flick on the porch light and set the table before my husband gets home. Over dinner, I will ask my men about their day, knowing that if only we could find the words, everyone would have a story as mysterious as mine. Later, as I handle tasks no one else really notices, the circus will begin its evening performance. The Hula Hoop Hero will try his luck again, the clown will choose his next apprentice. Someone in the crowd may witness a miracle, if not here tonight, then tomorrow, in the next town. Outside the circus enclosure, I am once again aware of the grass underfoot as I follow the crowd hurrying to their cars. Overhead, a flock of shouting crows swoops in the tent of the sky.

A LITTLE LOUDER, PLEASE

MAYBE I'M GOING DEAF. THOSE YULETIDE TV ADS ARE LOUDER and more compelling than the shows they're interrupting, but I don't seem to be hearing the message. December is swinging into its second week and I haven't bought any presents. Last weekend, my husband wrestled the tree into the living room and wrapped it with lights, but if that's as far as we get, I'm not going to be heartbroken about it. At night with those little lights glowing, you almost forget the ornaments are missing.

These are my dark ages. My kids are too old to believe in Santa and too young to give me grandchildren. They stopped caring about trees and holiday trappings about the time we gave in to their dad's allergies and went artificial. As far as their gifts are concerned, there are only so many ways you can wrap money. My husband likes to order his own gifts, and all I really want are my closets emptied and my left eyelid to stop sagging enough to let me see out of it in the morning. I'm not inspired to do much baking. Everyone my age knows about the dangers of letting

Christmas cookies into the house.

A few days ago, a three-year-old took me to lunch. Her mother drove, but the little queen was obviously in charge. Giuliana, dressed like a Victorian monarch in her flouncy skirt and short velvet cape, issued orders from her crash-tested throne in the back seat.

"A little louder, please," she said, indicating the car stereo. The queen's mum, like any good mother, pretended to comply by touching the volume knob.

"A little louder, please," our sovereign commanded again, with only a trace of irritation in her voice. Soon, such seasonal favorites as "All I want for Christmas is My Two Front Teeth" and "Frosty the Snowman" engulfed us.

I'm sure Giuliana's mother worried I might condemn her daughter's musical tastes as well as her own lack of parental control. On the contrary. A sappy rendition of "Jingle Bells" took me back to yuletides past when my own kids demanded the volume cranked on *Dr. Demento's Christmas Novelties*, payback for having tortured my own parents back in the day. As a child, my favorite weapon had been an album showcasing Jack Benny's halting violin and someone loudly lisping, "I thaw Mommy kithing Thanta Cloth." Little ones really do know what Christmas is all about.

"A little louder, please," the Good Queen said once more, this time, for our benefit. She wasn't having any trouble singing along with a relentlessly cheery "Deck the Halls." She wanted to be sure we heard the music, too. Her mom and I were so busy dissecting the past and worrying about the future, we were completely missing out on the *fa la la la la*.

A wiser woman would have joined in on a couple of verses of "The Twelve Days of Christmas" or "Rudolph the Red-Nosed Reindeer." I'm sorry, Giuliana. I wasn't ready to listen.

But it's not too late. Sadly, my own collection of holiday music is heavy on such hits as "The Holly and the Ivy," "O, Come, O, Come, Emmanuel," and carols played on antique German music boxes. But maybe if I get them playing loudly enough, I'll start to remember what the fuss is all about.

CRAB SURPRISE

M Y HUSBAND COMES BACK FROM ERRANDS WEARING A LOOK that tells me he's found something too good to pass up. "You'll never guess what I got," he says, and he's right. It's a crab net, only $19.95. He says it's a gift for our fifteen-year-old son.

This crab net is for the boy who would have happily spent every day of our Hawaiian vacation inside playing computer games. Like many teenaged boys, he prefers his hunting on a video screen. His eighteen-year-old brother is similarly inclined.

Our boys are not into seafood. They turn up their noses at the fresh abalone their father and his college buddy risk their lives to collect. With the Pacific less than twenty miles away, we have made many attempts to spark our sons' interest in the ocean. This trap is looking like a last-ditch effort, soon to be moldering in the garage, like all the wetsuits and other unused beach equipment.

But today, my husband, in that seemingly offhanded way men have, manages to catch this child when he's so bored he'll try anything. After one of those brief, monosyllabic exchanges I find unintelligible, the two of them agree that a little crabbing might be fun. Without further ado, the hunters prepare to set out, a few aging turkey hot dogs as their bait.

"Crab tonight!" I sing out as they load their equipment into the station wagon. The February air is warm, the sun dazzling. "Did you pack any sunscreen?" They choose to ignore the question.

"We might not catch anything," my husband warns.

"I'm not even sure I like crab," our son says.

"This will be a perfect time to find out," I say. "Even if you don't have any luck, you can always pick some up at the wharf."

I wonder if they can hear the slightly forced note in my nonchalance. My fondness for crab meat does not mean that I am entirely comfortable with crabs. I grew up only a few hours from the ocean, but in our farming town near Sacramento, Mom's crab feeds were even more exotic than her smoked oysters on crackers or avocados slices served with toothpicks, a dash of reconstituted lemon juice, and salt.

Mom must have gotten her crabs at the grocery store, though I don't remember seeing them behind the chilled glass of the butcher counter. Maybe I avoided the meat aisle on those trips, since the sight of crabs in their entirety has always frightened me a little. Like guns, crabs seem harmless only after they are taken apart.

Cracked crab was a special treat at our house, in part because it made for a noisy dinner, full of the sounds of snapping shells and our struggles to extricate the pale, juicy meat with nutpicks or fingers. It was delicious fare, but messy, a meal better suited for the outdoors, like watermelon or barbeque. But crab only appeared in the season of long sleeves, which we were always advised to roll up before we began to feast. Sometimes my mother tried to get me and my brother to wear giant plastic bibs left over from a couple of Kiwanis crab feeds she and Dad had attended. We always declined.

I remember a long-ago day at the ocean when my brother and I, ages nine and ten, dunked a borrowed crab trap baited with peanut butter sandwiches into the salty, sand-clouded water off the Dillon Beach dock. We never had to cultivate a fisherman's patience, because whenever we pulled the trap out of the water, we always found it bristling with greedy crustaceans, some even dangling on the outside of the netting. My brother was the only one brave enough to touch the beasts, but rather than flaunting his power, he simply allowed me to admire the way he caught them from behind and dropped them in our bucket of seawater.

Even though my husband and son aren't watching, I stand outside waving until our station wagon disappears at the bottom of the hill. I imagine my two crabbers heading toward their own kind of fun, though I wonder what has changed since that balmy winter afternoon with my brother. The neighbor tells me that at low tide forty years ago, he used to harvest abalone off the rocks and that even clams and mussels are scarce nowadays. I picture a few uneventful hours in which my husband judiciously throws back a few undersized critters before stopping at the Lucas Wharf for a freshly cracked Dungeness.

I am more than a little surprised when they come roaring in at five o'clock with wind-brightened eyes and cheeks, announcing they've caught five and bought two. Seven crabs for our family of four, all of them among the living.

"That's fabulous," I say, my stomach doing little flips at the sound of claws scraping against the sides of two covered pails on the back porch. I'm all for eating crab, but I haven't been thinking about killing it.

I admit I've gotten squeamish about my meat as the years go by. Gone from my grocery list are the pimply-skinned whole chickens of my childhood, the kind that came with necks and giblets, which my mother cut up, breaded, and fried along with the bony backs, breasts, and thighs. I don't know if my kids have even seen a chicken neck or gizzard, much less eaten one. Gone is the plate in the center of the table for all the bones that accumulated during a meal of chicken, ribs or fish. I can't imagine roasting marrowbones the way my mother did and convincing our boys to enjoy the creamy paste in their centers. I know better than to try to serve them liver.

Of course, my parents never tried to feed me calves' brains, tongue, kidneys, sweetbreads, Rocky Mountain, oysters, or other savage delicacies from their youths. For this I am grateful, but it's sad to realize I've denied my children wishbones. The girl who sometimes wished for nothing more than to win that after-dinner contest, who relished the crisp fried skins of trout and chicken, now wants her meat skinless, boneless, fat-free, and packaged in plastic. And her children have followed suit.

Those irritable creatures clicking their claws on the back porch remind me that if I confine myself to eating only what I am willing to kill and butcher, I am eliminating everything with hooves or beaks. Even fish above a certain size unnerve me. I could handle trout but would have to give up tuna. Even if I didn't quail at the notion of murdering a squid, I wouldn't have the energy to clean one.

Most days, I forget my cowardice when I'm standing in front of the deli counter, pointing to the sausages and lunchmeat I want to serve my family. But here are seven crabs fated to die whether we eat them or not. The hunters in this household have done their duty. There's nothing left but to fill my two largest pots with water and put them on the stove.

A secret signal must be transmitted when the water comes to a rolling boil, because everyone, including our oldest son, who declines to eat seafood in any form, shows up for the kill. As we peer into the beady eyes of our next meal, my husband and I mumble clumsy prayers of thanks for the impending sacrifice. It seems the least we can do.

The five little rock crabs caught off the Doran Beach jetty are waiting for their fate. All eyes are upon me as I approach their bucket with the barbeque tongs. I click my metal claw like the Castanets of Death and try to look like I'm having fun. After the first three drop listlessly into the bubbling water, I suggest that my youngest finish the job. There is a moment when I wonder if I've exhausted his tolerance for this enterprise, but he calmly dispatches the next two with no signs of excess glee or outward disgust.

The second pot is for the pair of Dungeness crabs bought at Lucas Wharf who spent the ride home trying to tear their way out of the paper they were wrapped in. They are twice the size of the others and fierce enough to make us wonder what we'd do if either of them got loose. At the sight of their waving claws, three of us turn silently to the head of the household, acknowledging that when there's dirty work to be done, it takes a real man to do it.

These crabs put up a magnificent fight. One in particular resists until the bitter end, hooking a couple of its jointed legs over the edge of the pot, refusing to go down. But after my hero assaults it with a pot lid, the last monster is subdued, and soon all shells are boiled to a satisfying rosiness. In a final gesture of gallantry, my husband cracks the crabs and piles them in a large bowl.

Cracked crab isn't something you can approach with hesitation. I watch the youngest, who usually doesn't like to get his hands dirty, quickly learn to twist the joints and use a nutcracker to break open the sturdy claws and legs. He doesn't seem to mind crab juice tracing itchy rivulets down his arms.

The work of our eating slows us down, and gives the crab hunters time to talk of their adventures. "We almost lost the trap first thing," our son says.

"But that kid who went in the water and got it for us," says his dad, "he was a human Labrador!"

The pile of emptied shells is soon higher than the remains of the uneaten. Even though I know he is probably full, our youngest picks up a Dungeness claw. "Remember how the guy at the wharf just reached into that tank full of crabs with his bare hands?" he muses. As he pulls on the bony tendon that works the claw joint, I hear raucous laughter of gulls and the slap of waves.

The smell of drying kelp reaches out to me from afternoons stretching all the way back to my childhood.

"Next time we'll get more people to help us eat all this crab," I say, using a nutpick to tease delicate white flesh from one last piece of the honeycombed body.

"No next time for me," laughs the oldest. He's made do with a ham sandwich for dinner, but he smiles when the rest of us nod, anticipating the taste of our future.

LETTING GO

I long, as does every human being, to be at home wherever I find myself.   —Maya Angelou

LEAVING
THE VALLEY

BECAUSE MY MOTHER IS RECOVERING FROM SURGERY, I DRIVE THE eighty miles to my hometown without the added commotion of my husband and kids. It's only an overnight stay, more for form's sake than to offer any significant aid. I bring along a few frozen casseroles, a bottle of scented hand lotion, and a bouquet from the grocery store, certain that Mom and Dad have planned for and taken care of the rest. Although this is no occasion to celebrate, I'm looking forward to this late summer visit. Now that I have my own family, I'm rarely alone with my parents anymore.

I pull into the spot my father has saved for me on the driveway, and step out of my air-conditioned station wagon. Although momentarily stunned by the furnacing valley heat, I am grateful to be away from the breezy temperance of the coast, where August afternoons at the public pool can turn my children's lips blue. My body is eager to adopt the insolent slouch, the lazy squint of other summers I've known in this hard, dry heat. I immediately begin to feel lighter, less oppressed, knowing that if I were to go swimming in a neighbor's pool, the water beads would whisper off my body into the silence of sun-warmed air.

In the coolness of the dim, neat kitchen, my breath takes on an older cadence; I move to rhythms remembered from childhood. I miss the sounds of my mother bustling among the appliances, but while she rests in the bedroom, wrapped in motionless sleep, my father and I take up our old positions on stools at the counter. As he talks, Dad picks up a mechanical pencil to sketch some shelves he is designing, while I let myself relax into the pauses between his words.

Without my husband to look askance, I drink glass after glass of bitter iced tea made with the briny softened water he refuses to drink. Without the presence of my children, Dad and I snack too much, just as we used to, enjoying with childish delight the crunch of countless pretzels, the sweet chill of ice cream bars.

In the evening, my mother joins us on the patio as we listen to the heavy saw of crickets working under the scented jasmine. We all secretly miss the cigarettes we've recently given up, one more of the ceremonies my other family disapproves of. Later, I lie alone in my old room, hearing through the open window the distant clatter of night harvesters, lumbering in clouds of luminous dust along the tomato furrows. I waken to the faint rustle of moon-brightened leaves, and again, just before dawn, to the hiss of sprinklers feathering the lawn.

As planned, I head home early the next day. A few short blocks, and I'm driving through the plowed fields that lap against the edge of town. I barrel down straight-shot county roads named with numbers and laid out at right angles over miles of absolute flatness. A choking tenderness causes me to roll down all the windows in the car so that I'm washed in my native air—cooler today than any remembered August morning.

The buffeting air brings long-familiar scents to me. My throat tightens on the fierce tang of dust, heat-blown tomatoes, crushed stalks, fertilizer. A few farm houses squat among the tomato fields or hide behind fences of ripening corn. I pass acres of thistly safflower, already autumnal bronze, and battalions of heavy-headed sunflowers the size of dinner plates. Here, the alfalfa has just been cut, and countless pale butterflies bobble among its fading greeness or batter themselves against my front grill. Now and then I catch the mossy smell of water in softly falling irrigation spills or scattered like shards of mirror around bristling shoots of green rice. I see the highway, miles distant, where big rigs and motor homes roll in steady silence along the base of sand-colored foothills.

Suddenly, the road I travel rises in a dizzying arc that follows no geographical contour. This overpass marks the end of what I consider my home ground. As I climb the shimmering onramp to join the urgent traffic, the last bits of my childhood blow back and away out the car windows. Tears blur my vision for a moment, and then I am driving toward my real life again.

LAST SUPPER

I*T ISN'T LIKE SHE'S DEAD OR ANYTHING, I TELL MYSELF. JANE IS only moving.* But that bit of pedestrian logic, topped with a wealth of good reasons for Jane's out-of-state exodus, does not ease the constriction in my throat as I drive to her house for a goodbye party.

I weathered the rash of mid-life divorces that hit my circle a few years back. I survived the shock of sending my oldest son off to college. Lately, I have begun to brace myself for the decline and fall of all four parents in our family and the last of their siblings. But Jane's departure is hitting me hard. Maybe some of my grief has to do with the fact that Jane is the fifth good friend this year to move out of the area, with a sixth scheduled to depart in a few months. I feel as though no one thought to warn me about this particular thinning of the ranks. It doesn't help to remind myself that the cost of living in California makes it a tough place to get old or start over.

I am one of the first to arrive at Jane's and, as I watch the steady stream of friends, neighbors, and coworkers arriving through the green front door to pay their respects, I see I'm not the only one having a tough time of it. Everyone enters smiling and full of upbeat chatter, but there is a dazed look about them, as if they can't quite figure out what to do next.

So we attack the food. This is a natural reaction at one of Jane's parties. Her spreads are legendary, and even though she faces her last hectic week as events coordinator for a local bookstore and has a houseful of cats and furniture to move in less than ten days, she has still managed to prepare three pork roasts with different marinades, mountains of buffalo wings, pasta salad, a frittata with fresh artichoke hearts, plates of fresh fruit, apple bread, sausages, breads, and cheeses, all of it beautifully presented and absolutely delicious. Jane is someone who holds the torch of hospitality high and beckons to the poor and huddled masses yearning to eat freely. Today she has a new way to dismiss her generosity: *Cooking is easier than packing.*

And eating is easier than thinking. We all load up our plates and feast, gazing out the many windows of Jane's house at views of the open space preserve that laps like a grassy ocean nearly into her living room. Jane and some of her neighbors were instrumental in saving this particular piece of wildness from developers, and so every red-shouldered hawk and wild turkey we spot going about its business among the oaks and brambles feels like Jane's gift to us.

Jane has been a tireless guardian of the preserve, willing to confront anyone who disrupts the fragile peace of the animals' habitat: kids with paintball guns and dirt bikes, dog owners unwilling to put their pets on leashes, even bands of homeless who bring the danger of fire to the property. One of her neighbors says, a little mournfully, *I hope the next owners of this house will take care of the land.*

I murmur my approval of that sentiment, but what I'm really thinking is, *Who will take care of me after Jane leaves?* I remember all those times Jane made me comfortable in this house of airy vistas by encouraging me to make a pig of myself with all her good cooking. It wasn't ever anything my body needed, god knows, but Jane always managed to feed my soul.

At Jane's I become one of those terrible guests who never helps with the cleanup. I've always let her make a fuss over me, which she's managed to do without ever appearing in the least bit strained. Plus, she's always made sure I knew about all the really great book signings and literary events in the area, and she's gifted me with advanced readers' copies of books that have become favorites. She fed my desire last year to keep chickens by supplying me with books, chicken portraits, placemats, and even rooster cocktail picks during the long months my project was delayed. That's why I have brought her one of the tiny brown eggs one of my three hens has just started laying—Jane totally gets it.

I know this isn't the end of our friendship. We have all the tools, both ancient and modern, to keep in touch. California isn't even that far from Oregon—we can visit each other. I know it's selfish to place so much value on what someone like Jane can do for me. But I can't be the only one who feels the impending sorrow behind this final meal together. We are all eating more than we even want to, letting Jane feed us one last time.

PICTURES DON'T

LAND'S END, CORNWALL, ENGLAND —MY MOTHER POSES FOR my camera on a rickety suspension bridge, here at this place called Land's End. She lifts her chin, trying to ignore the buffeting wind that tugs at her scarf and sets the rope bridge swaying. The sky on this late September morning is blue but darkening. Another storm brewing. I watch her through my viewfinder as she steadies herself over the boulder-strewn chasm. When I pull back the zoom, trying to capture the scope of the scene, she looks suddenly small, far away. I see her hesitate before she smiles.

September babies, we have both just had our birthdays. Mom turned seventy-one as we packed for this trip. I slipped into my forty-fifth year during our flight from SFO to Heathrow. The two of us can hardly believe we are finally spending two weeks together in England, so we take each other's pictures for proof. Or rather, I take my mother's picture, because she usually forgets about the one-use camera buried at the bottom of her fanny pack. "Don't worry about it, Mom," I say, a little impatiently, when she starts digging past her reading glasses, sunglasses, Wash 'N Dries, breath mints. I gesture with my old Canon to wave her into position. "You can do it next time."

I am the daughter of a woman who believes in looking her best in any situation. On that score, this trip has been a challenge. For starters, we have allowed ourselves only one carry-on and tote apiece. On our daily outings, we are lumpy with all the money belts, fanny packs, water bottles, gloves, scarves, cameras, maps, bus passes, extra glasses, brochures, and souvenirs we keep about our persons. Our travel umbrellas keep getting blown inside out, so we face the wind and weather in scarves knotted babushka style, or in goofy rain hats. We tramp across cathedral floors, pastures, and cobbled streets, our ankles splashed with mud, in shoes that can only be described as sensible.

"Another one of the old lady," Mom keeps saying, as if she wishes for a glamorous stand-in to prop in front of every beauty spot and monument. I've never heard my slender, stylish mother talk like this. In our unspoken code, looking good may be a goal, but it's never the subject of discussion. She's still a good sport and poses anyway, angling her shoulders and head the way her big sister Hattie taught her, the way she's tried to teach me.

I keep a framed hometown newspaper article and photo of Mom in my studio. It dates back almost forty years, and in it my mother faces the camera with sweet confidence, her dark hair a luxuriant cloud, her eyes set off by intelligently arched brows. It is a feature story from a simpler time. Our complete address is prominently displayed, along with her recipe for a salad of lime Jell-O, walnuts, canned pineapple, and cottage cheese. She laughed the first time she saw it on my desk. The recipe wasn't the only thing she found ridiculous. "I remember rushing to the newspaper office to get that picture taken. I don't even think I had time to comb my hair." I wonder if she has been remembering how easy it used to be to feel presentable, or if I ever told her she was as beautiful as Jackie Kennedy back then.

The wind gives the bridge a capricious shake. After her terrorized gasp, a look of nervous determination settles over Mom's face. It's an expression new to this trip, when unfamiliar stairs, curbs, accents, and exchange rates cause her to lose her bearings, slow her pace, cling to railings. I will see it tomorrow, among the ruins of gale-ravaged Tintagel, just after she slips on a muddy patch and goes down on both hands. We'll both laugh in the howling wind and rain and wipe the mud off her palms with Kleenex, but a little later, posing her in the shelter of an ancient slate guardhouse, her face will look pale as I focus the camera.

A few evenings ago, at a concert in Oxford, an older man asked if we were grandmother and granddaughter. "We're *sisters*," I'd hissed with a witchy smile, delighting in his resulting embarrassment. There may have been a time when I wanted proof of my ascendancy over my mother; now I want us on equal footing. Instead, I find myself warning her to watch for cars and taking her hand while crossing the street. I pluck coins from her cupped palm when she is slow counting change. I choose where we stay and what we see. I am pleased with myself at how smoothly everything has been going. But I also feel presumptuous, more than a little bossy. Because she is willing to defer to me, I even decide when to take her picture, forcing her to stand on derelict bridges, cajoling her into smiling a little harder.

"You have to keep fighting the urge to give up," she says ✎ that night over a heaping plate of pub food in the harbor town of Penzance. She is referring to the gradual betrayals of her aging body, a capricious memory, and recently diagnosed cataracts. There's an assortment of pills she discreetly takes each day for ailments we avoid discussing. Our mother-daughter trip is now more than half over. I can see that she's happy and tired and how much she trusts me. After I've settled the bill, I'll ask her to take my picture in front of the restaurant. When my photos arrive from the developers, my mother will look radiant in each one.

GETTING A RIDE

FOR THE MOST PART, MY HUSBAND AND I UNDERSTAND THAT marriage is a small boat, and, as the years go by, we have learned not to rock it. He asks, "Everything okay?" I answer, "Sure. No problem." But one afternoon, in a fit of mild boredom, I decided to treat the next question he asked like something of real importance. Oddly enough, this turned out to be, "So, what kind of car would you like to drive?"

I have to tell you that I'm a forty-six-year-old woman who has spent her entire motoring career behind the wheels of vehicles some man thought she ought to be driving. It started with one of my father's hand-me-downs, a faded blue Datsun 1200, which I drove with indifference during my last years of college and on into my first teaching job. In the back of my mind, I kept thinking the old rattletrap would die, and then I'd buy something I really wanted.

Before that could happen, I married a man with strong opinions about things like engine reliability, aerodynamics, and fuel economy. He has always thought my car should say certain things about me, although we've never agreed on what those things should be. Just before the Datsun gave up the ghost, he bought me a Volkswagen Rabbit. Ten years ago, with the kids getting bigger, I was installed in a Ford Taurus station wagon. Now it was time for a new car, so his question was big, one that could change everything. "I'll have to think about it," I said.

To my surprise, he said he'd wait. In the meantime, he took me to see Audi A4s and Volkswagen Passats. I understood I was supposed to thrill at their understated elegance, the solid slam of their doors, those side air bags and high crash-test ratings. Intellectually, I could appreciate his good taste and concern for quality, his wish to see his family safe and pampered. But I remained unmoved and undecided.

I found myself squinting at every car that passed on the freeway, trying to figure out what it was I didn't like about them. Some had hysterically pitched windshields, or back ends that were all waggling and rude, like the wrong kind of woman in a thong bikini. The cars I was seeing had all the appeal of empty aluminum cans.

I remembered those classy Karmann Ghias and Mercedes 450 SLs I'd yearned for back in my dim and ill-spent youth. Surely, there was something out there now, maybe even in my price range, that expressed my current world view. One day, while the kids were in school, I got into my station wagon and headed to our town's auto row. I felt shifty as a petty criminal dreaming up a scheme, because as soon as I drove by the Ford dealership, the notion of driving a muscly American car suddenly began to appeal to me. I wanted to know what it would feel like to drive something named after a swift or mythical beast—Mustang, Viper, Firebird, Impala—or warm seaside places like Daytona, Riviera, LeMans, Malibu. I was going someplace I was not supposed to be, the wrong side of the road, the other side of the tracks.

Then I saw it: a white Chrysler Sebring convertible with a black ragtop. It's more ferryboat than sports car, built for leisurely adventure or a luxurious commute. It's a car designed for the moment you tilt your chin to the sun and let fly a laugh. With this car, I'd have to pay serious attention to vista points and scenic highways. I'd have to keep scarves and little sweaters and sunscreen handy. Without a solid roof and layers of respectability to hide behind, I'd have to be prepared for people looking at me, to have children whose mom doesn't drive a station wagon anymore.

Well, of course my husband cringed when I told him about the Sebring, but this time I didn't laugh and make like I didn't know what I was talking about. Even if I ended up in a dreaded minivan, I decided to act like a woman who drives a convertible, someone who's learned that knowing what you want is half of who you are.

Suddenly, I could see myself behind the wheel with the top down, my hair in a big scarf, Jackie-O sunglasses obscuring the lines around my eyes. It's a bright warm afternoon, of course, and there's a bossa nova playing just loud enough on the stereo. I'm on my way to someplace interesting, and I have a husband sitting next to me who doesn't quite know who I am anymore. But he wants to know, and he's asking.

BOXED IN

LOTS OF THINGS BOTHER ME ABOUT GETTING OLDER—HOW THE print on menus and product labels disappears in dim light, how the kitchen timer is no longer loud enough to catch my attention, how I don't seem to have any eyebrows any more. My friends are starting to make Alzheimer jokes, and we admit it's getting harder to drive at night. All these little betrayals are really starting to pile up, like all the boxes in my dining room.

It seems like every week or so a box will be delivered to our front porch, courtesy of all the money-and-energy-saving shopping we do with catalogs and the Internet. My family receives shipments of vitamins, spa equipment, clothes, and books, as well as bike, car, and electronic parts, all of which arrive in sturdy cartons. Often these purchases involve two boxes—one to contain the shoes, for example, another to hold the shoebox.

Someone around here is always willing to open the boxes and scatter the invoices, wads of packing paper, Styrofoam peanuts, and bubble wrap. But no one ever volunteers to break the boxes into manageable, recyclable hunks. They're everywhere, piling up in the dining room like the sandstone blocks of the Great Pyramid at Giza. I don't see this happening at my friends' houses. How do they do it? Are they stronger than I am? Better household managers? I'm overwhelmed and more than a little embarrassed. I'd hide the suckers in the garage if it weren't already full.

I worry that boxes are getting tougher, resistant to destruction the way streptococcus is becoming impervious to antibiotics. These days, my tee shirts and used books are being shipped in containers that could survive a trip over Niagara Falls. The prospect of kicking them flat or carving them up with a box cutter exhausts me. Online shopping shouldn't be an aerobic activity. And it feels dangerous. One slip of the blade and there goes my finger.

Unfortunately, when it comes to boxes, my husband and I have philosophical differences that go beyond the division of labor. My mate has a live-and-let-live approach to the plain brown behemoths tossed around our house like accent pillows. If someone wants to deal with them, fine. If not, just leave them on the coffee table.

In addition, he reveres the original boxes of every small appliance, stereo component or computer part we possess and adamantly refuses to part with them. As long as we own the printer or the toaster oven, he likes to keep the box handy—just in case. Never mind that we haven't moved in twenty-two years and General Electric won't service our seventeen-year-old microwave any more. With boxes, it's better to be safe than sorry.

I have a fondness for containers myself. I'm constantly expanding my collection of baskets, jars, vases, crates. I am the lifeblood of stores with names like "Hold Everything." If my husband develops a yen for some little containers to store nails and washers, he'll collect baby food jars from the neighbor. If he wants to get fancy, he'll soak off the labels. But I want even the utilitarian to be ornamental. In that way I'm like my mother, who keeps her plastic corn-on-the-cob holders in a box she covered with seashell wallpaper in 1953. Then there was the Christmas she turned all our empty soup and juice cans into candle holders. My mate does not get the urge to own a cookie jar or a special dispenser for stamps. But I have given friends pretty boxes as gifts, even with nothing in them.

I value ugly boxes if they are storing something special, like ski clothes, baby pictures, or old letters. I keep Christmas ornaments in some that once belonged to my grandmother, who knew a good box when she saw one. Every afghan or tablecloth or pair of slippers she made as a gift would be presented in a perfectly proportioned box. I still wonder what happened to the white pasteboard box in her kitchen drawer that fit a stack of square paper napkins *exactly*. I wonder if she was genetically predisposed to find that kind of thing satisfying.

Then there are gift boxes. They don't make these like they used to anymore, and that's okay, because I have stockpiles that go back decades. My mother specializes in those embossed with the names of stores that no longer exist. She and I try to keep these treasures in the family, and we enjoy a sentimental thrill whenever we can pass them back and forth to each other. We also have a thing about old ribbon, but that's another story.

The boxes that currently threaten to engulf me are neither charming nor specifically geared toward any item in our possession. They are not original or pretty or sentimental, but it still seems almost sinful to throw them away. Perhaps this is because an empty cardboard box is all about potential. What if we finally decide to send my cousin a baby gift, or sell some junk on EBay? What if we need a bed for a lost puppy or a hot casserole dish that might spill in the car otherwise? It's not like in the old days when you could find good boxes at the back door of any grocery store. What would happen if we had to move? Then we'd be sorry for all those boxes we threw away.

I think this is how elderly people who fill their houses with newspapers and tuna fish cans and balls of aluminum foil get started. Given the right circumstances, they think, old rubber bands, plastic bags and pieces of string might prove useful. The day may come when I start feeling the same way about boxes. In the event of an earthquake, I could fashion a shelter out of them. Find one the right size, it would make a great coffin.

GIFT EXCHANGE

"**W**HAT DO YOU WANT FOR CHRISTMAS?" MY HUSBAND asked as he hung the last of my grandmother's crocheted snowflakes on our everlasting PVC tree. I fiddled with a pipe cleaner angel, considering my answer; we only had ten shopping days to make it happen.

What I really wanted was for him to clean out the garage, but I knew where that request would get me. "Those fleece-lined boots we saw downtown would be nice," I finally replied. "So, when are you going to tell me what you want?"

From the way he looked off into the distance, I suspected he had his own list of unspoken desires. "I'm working on it," he said.

The thrill isn't gone, exactly. It's just that as the years go by, we continue to downsize the holidays. Gone forever are the displays of lavishly wrapped affection piled at the base of our now fake Tannenbaum, the orgies of Christmas carbs, and the superhero known as Santa Claus. There's relief in being practical.

Besides, after twenty-seven years at the same address, we're at that stage where getting new stuff isn't nearly as important as dealing with what we already have. We've got a house needing paint and new windows, a furnace on its last legs, a filled-to-bursting garage, and two kids in college. We also have to fight the tide of decay in our aging pets and parents, not to mention our own increasingly unreliable bodies, while our sons do what they can to move out from under our grip.

What we really want for Christmas is more time for ourselves and the people we love. It's not something we've discussed much, but lately, whenever we've managed to step off the hamster wheel of duty and work, we've noticed how the larger world can spin at a slower rate than previously imagined.

There really is time to discover new museums and restaurants, take in a theater performance or hike, buy curly kale at the biodynamic produce stand, brew a batch of beer, have friends over for dinner, watch the chickens, write a letter, and maybe even plan a vacation. Contrary to the way it feels sometimes, how we use our lives is really up to us.

Yesterday, I woke up just before my alarm went off. The world felt so dark and cold, I cowered there under the covers dreading all the work waiting for me. But then, without a word, George got up, fed the cat, and began a purposeful rattle of pans in the kitchen. Soon the aroma of ham and eggs had Dante out of his own warm bed for his early morning junior college class. All the while, I got to lie there in my downy cocoon, counting my blessings as winter dawnlight filled the room. The garage didn't seem like a very big deal, especially when my list of blessings included a tree decorated with a man who'd soon be placing gifts for me under it.

I'm sure we'll manage to scrape together an assortment of presents to open on Christmas. The ritual exchange of boots, books, tools, and woolies is one of those traditions we seem determined to cling to. But this year, I want time to hold the place of honor under the tree. It's a gift we can give and enjoy every day, and comes with ribbons long enough to keep us tied to everybody and everything.

THE VERY AIR

I ALWAYS NOTICE THE SMELLS OF THE SURROUNDING FIELDS WHEN I turn off the 505 north of Winters and head east on Yolo county blacktop toward my hometown of Woodland, California. In winter, the odor of rain-soaked earth dominates; in spring the greening, blossoming almond orchards and apple green rice shoots overpower all else. As summer builds toward fall, the tang of fertilizer and tomato vines is slowly taken over by discarded tomatoes rotting in the fields or smashed flat and baking on the asphalt.

But the atmosphere in my parents' home, where they've lived for thirty years, is a changeless thing—a biosphere that contains an immutable combination of scents, no matter what the season. I could not identify the ingredients, except to say that the mixture reminds me of the sanded planks in my father's woodshop and the dried stalks of statice my mother occasionally arranges on the dining room table. Even though it's getting more difficult for me to relax around my father, who is not aging gracefully, I am still able to breathe in a sense of deep calm whenever I enter their house.

When I was a kid living in a smaller house near the Yolo County Fairgrounds, I knew and anticipated the cellar-like coolness of my friend Jolie's house, or the lemon-waxed and freshly ironed atmosphere that prevailed at Becky's, where an African American woman in a white uniform obeyed the orders of Becky's Mississippi-born mother. In those days, the scent I now associate with my parents may have been lost in a welter of my father's cigarette smoke, the musky kiss of my mother's Estèe Lauder, and the aromas of cooking: sauerkraut with anise seeds, percolated coffee, fried chicken, or pot roast. Our home's trademark scent, for there must have been one, made no impression on me. It went unnoticed, as unremarkable as the oatmeal or soft-boiled eggs and toast my mother placed on the Formica-topped kitchen table on winter mornings.

It is just my mom and dad, now, without the moil of my brother and me swirling the air with activities and secrets. I wonder if my parents resented their children's unruly smells back then, if their nostrils recoiled from that stink as mine sometimes do from the foxy scent my sons' rooms accumulate. I like to think my parents savored the hints of the deodorants or colognes Warren and I used to wear, or walked into clouds of recently abandoned shower steam and inhaled greedily, hoping to keep forever that particular combination of soap, toothpaste, and shampoo, just as I find myself doing after the boys' ablutions.

What mystifies me is the way the smells of my parents, so harmonious and unobtrusive in their own home, wreak havoc with my nose when they come to visit us. The two of them sleep on the hide-a-bed in my office and use the bathroom that adjoins it. Granted, I consider these rooms mine, but I never think of myself as possessive when other people visit. It's my father, in particular, who imbues the air with a penetrating odor of stagnation that can take days to shoo out. When he visits it's as if I can sniff, with a dog's certainty, all that he has been unable to digest, both spiritually and physically. Dad has marked a kind of territory for himself with his stubborn refusal to exercise or make changes in his diet, while the whiff of stale perfume that lingers in the wake of my mother's visits is another reminder of her growing frailty and her continued efforts to put up a gracious front.

But perhaps my parents can't bring their home scent with them. The sharp odors that cling to our guest room blinds are probably the result of the difficulty they have traveling these days. The distance between our houses is only eighty miles, but they always take a break halfway at a McDonald's or a Denny's and time their drive to avoid nightfall and weekend traffic. Our house is drafty and dusty, with unavoidable stairs. The coastal air of Petaluma is always damp, and without the familiar comforts of a favorite robe, a properly placed reading light, and larders and medicine chests whose contents are deeply known, my parents pack an air of uncertainty along with their toothbrushes.

Friends talk of the way their dead parents have returned to them in dreams, but more often, in the form of a distinctive aroma—the scent of rosewater in a grocery aisle, or the smell of burning pipe tobacco in an otherwise empty car. I wonder which scent, if any, my parents will one day choose as manifestations. I hope they will signal their presence with the familiar atmosphere of calm that reminds me of the clear light of an afternoon sky in winter. It is the smell of the home they have always kept ready for me, my home once, and part of me forever.

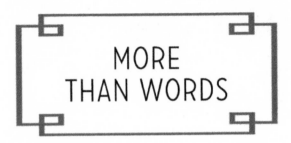

MORE
THAN WORDS

I WISH I COULD TELL YOU SOME OF THE STORIES MY SEVENTY-
eight-year-old mother tells me. But I'd have to remember her
words, which unspool from her mouth like a piece of yarn pulled
loose from a sweater. These words are often sweet and hugely
funny, but they rarely lodge in my memory, maybe because stories
depend on context, and for Mom, the context keeps changing.
Sometimes I am her daughter, sometimes a kindly stranger;
sometimes the bathroom door is the size of a postage stamp;
sometimes a dark tile is a hole in the floor. She'll tell me about
the children who follow her everywhere, the man my father has
agreed to let her marry, or the time the cowboys on rodeo horses
rode through her room in the memory care unit. No matter how
her world changes, Mom keeps talking, pulling on that kinked
thread, as if by doing so she can follow it back to the woman she
used to be.

When taking apart a piece of knitting, your attention fixes
on the edge that is unraveling. You become fascinated by the blur
of movement and changing shape at the place where form

collapses. That line of tucks and loops bears no resemblance to the garment worn on a hundred winter afternoons. Soon it's just a stringy tangle pooling in your lap.

These days, my mother's voice is soft and wooly. It wraps itself around the control panel in my brain so I can't see which knob to turn to help me figure out what I really need to know. Looking up at me from a gurney while we wait for the ER doctor to give us a report on her recent fall, she tries to tell me what happened in the three hours before I could get to the hospital. "My head hurt," she says, "so I asked the nurse for a pickle."

She laughs, so we both know this isn't what she meant to say. "Did you mean 'pillow'?" I ask, and she beams at my perspicacity. In this moment, her story makes perfect sense. Then she says, "Just because I can't walk, doesn't mean I can't shake." And I am plunged into mystery.

Nothing in my experience has prepared me for this, except maybe those long-ago days of colic, fevers, and teething when I'd done everything I could think of to make my babies comfortable and still they cried and cried. I know from those times the only real mistake is succumbing to despair or anger. This knowledge lets me ignore my mother's repeated requests to go to the bathroom, because the nurse who helped me get her dressed, into a wheelchair, out into the cold spring wind, and into my car has taken the wheelchair back into the hospital. No one is stepping in with a better strategy. Certainly not my ailing father, home asleep in his chair, who tells her she's just not concentrating, or my husband who told me it was crazy to drop everything and drive a hundred miles to the hospital when tomorrow or next week the real emergency might arrive.

After forty-five minutes in rush hour traffic, I get her to the toilet in the memory care facility, where she pees a thimbleful. Then I stand by as the staff puts her into bed in a room dim with twilight. When I tell her I have to get going, she teases, "Next time I might just weight you down with horseshoes so you can't leave."

"We have to stop talking now, Ma," I tell her. "Close your eyes. Get some rest." I sit on the edge of her bed, waiting until her eyes stop twitching beneath their lids. She sleeps. I concentrate on the small dark space between her parted lips where the stories come out, trying to prepare for the time when the words will stop.

A PIECE
OF THE PIE

D AD'S EIGHTY-FOURTH BIRTHDAY PARTY WAS GOING NICELY. I'D invited a bunch of his old friends for the afternoon celebration, and the house rang with convivial laughter the way it had in the days when Mom was hostess. I'd made a mince pie, Dad's favorite birthday treat, and Dad managed to blow out the four candles I decided to use, not easy for a man on an oxygen concentrator. Then it was time to serve up the aforementioned mince, a crumb-topped strawberry rhubarb pie from a local farm stand, and a cheesecake, courtesy of Trader Joe's.

I stood in the dining room with Ellie and Margaret, steadfast friends of my parents since the 1950s. "I wish Mom were here," I said, staring at the three as-yet untouched desserts. "I never did learn how to serve pie." Before Alzheimer's, cakes, pastries and candies were my mother's specialties. Not so long ago, she would have been here serving three picture perfect desserts she'd made from scratch. What's more, every portion, from first to last, would have been worthy of a photograph.

Ellie gave me a little squeeze, no doubt remembering her recent visit with Mom in the memory unit across town. "Sweetie, compared to your mom, none of us learned how."

I'm not sure where Mom learned the art of serving desserts. I never bothered to ask. Perhaps it was at her high school job at a soda fountain, or during her Chico State college days when she worked for room and board in the home of a well-to-do family. In those years, she volunteered on committees, joined a sorority and later a bridge club—all places where desserts were dished with style.

As a child, I believed the talent for serving pie was something you had to be born with, like a photographic memory or perfect pitch. I used to think she took dessert duty at every family function because no one, not my aunts or even my revered grandmother, had been blessed with the gift.

Later, as I careened through adolescence, I tried to dismiss my mother's abilities. Pie and cake cutting, if I thought about them at all, were techniques I would undoubtedly master with ease the moment I acquired the opportunity to practice them. After all, if Mom could do it, how hard could it be? After surviving some messy, embarrassing trials as a newlywed, I handed the knife back to my mother, who resumed her duties without comment or complaint.

It's ironic that much of what Mom did manage to teach me, skills like using laundry bluing, darning socks, or spreading liquid floor wax with a lamb's wool applicator, have gone the way of the buggy whip. I don't know why I didn't learn to imitate the gentle sawing motion she employed for angel food, the trial cuts she made in the air over a sheet cake as she calculated the number of servings, her tricks for keeping a cheesecake blade clean. Maybe because when it came to dessert, I thought she'd always be around to serve it.

As I slopped Dad's piece of mince onto a paper plate, I compared my effort against the memory of one of Mom's perfect wedges, showcased on her good china, garnished with hard sauce, a sterling dessert fork tucked beside it. At least Ellie and Margaret were close by, laughing along with me, looking the other way when I used my fingers, and, unlike Mom if she'd been there, refusing to let me give up.

"Your mom was in a class apart," Margaret said before she took loaded plates to the living room. "You're just going to have to settle for being one of us."

"Sounds like a plan," I said, remembering to divide the rhubarb pie in half before making the rest of the cuts. That made the going a little easier, and I let myself dare to imagine all the times Mom must have gotten pie filling on her fingers and frosting on her sleeve. She had to have suffered dropped forks, burned crusts, and fallen cakes, even before dementia began taking its ragged slices. In the next room, I heard approving murmurs as folks dug into their desserts. Without thinking too hard, I slipped my knife through the creamy center of the cheesecake like I'd been doing it all my life.

WINGS

"THAT'S QUITE A SACK OF ROCKS YOU'RE CARRYING, SWEETIE," my father's friend Bruce said more than once during phone calls in last year of Dad's life. It was his way of acknowledging how heavily Dad's hard-headedness and self-imposed isolation weighed on me. But I also took it as a tribute to Dad's stubbornness and a nod to my strength, too.

"Dumb as a rock" never made much sense to me. Stone strikes me as having its own unassailable intelligence. Its ability to endure illustrates its genius. I have never believed the ability to reckon calculus or produce sonnets was proof of intelligence, although I shared with Dad the idea that someone with rocks in his head was lacking in foresight and flexibility. Rocks may be smart, but they are slow. Time measured in stone is time lost to reason.

There were times during my dad's dying that were as slow as serpentine, sandstone, rose quartz, chert. His unseeing eyes were shiny blank obsidian, and the pauses between breaths were long enough to form fossils. But just after that great wave rolled down from the crown of his head, darkening the air around him so the spirit that remained glowed like a white pebble at the bottom of a silty river, a tear slid from beneath one of his closed eyelids. That's when the sack of rocks fell empty at my feet and I was surrounded by the tumult of released wings.

RECYCLING

I T'S A CLEAR AUGUST MORNING AT GLASS BEACH IN FORT BRAGG, California, a small stretch of coastline just north of Mendocino. Today, I'm here on a break between sessions at a writers' conference, just one of the many visitors skirting the edges of the breaking waves, amazed that the colorful gravel crunching underfoot is composed almost entirely of glass.

Glass Beach is neither miracle nor mystery, although it feels like both. The same waves grinding the lion-colored cliffs to sand have converted tons of Fort Bragg's discarded glass into small, smooth pebbles. On a day like this, the wet shore glitters with the remains of pulverized mayonnaise, medicine, and mason jars, green and amber liquor bottles, blue Noxzema and Milk of Magnesia containers, unidentified shards of amethyst and ruby, all washed clean as sun-bleached shells or driftwood. It's hard to connect this innocent sparkle with waste, but for nearly one hundred years, the townspeople brought their garbage to this edge of North America and dumped it into the Pacific.

Now, forty years later, people come like children to an Easter egg hunt. One man pours his collection of bright chips into a salvaged cigarette box; an older couple leans together, smiling at the contents of their cupped palms. Two young girls deposit their finds in a plastic bucket, chatting with their mother and their camera-wielding grandmother in what sounds like German.

Each time I come to Glass Beach I take a handful of its special glass to add to the bowlful I keep at home. But on this trip, even though there's a plastic bag tucked in my pocket, I'm in no mood for treasure hunting. My father has recently died, and my only brother, gaunt and confused, languishes in a rehab facility after a near-fatal car crash. My mother, confused in her own way, loses more of herself in a locked memory care unit. These days, my two adult sons, busy making lives for themselves, can be added to the list of loved ones who inhabit distant realms.

Instead of heading toward the water's edge, I clamber up a craggy bluff, clutching my paper cup of coffee with its plastic lid. I walk along the cliffs, willing the persistent rhythms of the ocean to calm my restless heart and lungs. When my foot slips on loose rock, nothing feels safe or connected.

I am alone. If I fell, unnoticed, into one of the craggy inlets along the continent's serrated edge, my cotton-and-wool-clad flesh would soon be consumed by crabs, gulls, and other shoreline scavengers. The breakdown of my bony parts would be a longer business, but the work of a moment compared to my hard plastic contact lenses, amalgam fillings, jewelry, and battery-operated watch, all of which feel as much a part of me as my eyelids or hair. Humans have always generated refuse, but what beauty could the waves make of my economy car parked at the trailhead, the lid to my coffee cup, or the polyvinyl soles of my shoes?

It's hard to think about garbage on a warm summer morning at the beach when people are smiling at each other and at me. Later, as I wander near the tideline, a teenaged girl approaches with a digital camera and asks me to take a picture of her with her family. "C'mon, everyone," she urges them, "we don't have any shots of the four of us."

I can see from the way the parents lean away from each other, this group was shipwrecked long ago, broken apart, all hands lost. But time has smoothed the sharp edges of that breaking and brought them ashore for this reunion at Glass Beach. The daughters stand together in the middle, arms linked, their free hands gathering their parents closer. Everyone surrenders, takes a deep breath and gives me a shy grin. "Beautiful!" I tell them as I press the shutter release.

Today, if I had a camera, what would I take pictures of? A swirl of glass confetti gleaming in a pocket of tide water, perhaps, or the lip of froth on the edge of a wave, but really, it's the enduring patience of the sea I want to capture, a force that works without prejudice to return to the elements anything we give it. When I finally start back up the dusty path toward my car, I'm empty-handed except for my plastic bag, which now contains my coffee cup and a few stray bits of modern litter.

As the trail takes me through blackberry brambles higher than my head, I hear snatches of a melody so faint, at first I think it's the ocean's roar carried forward on the breeze. The mournful singing is muffled by sand, rocks, and sun-warmed blackberry vines, and broken into fragments by waves of wind. Although I can't make out the words, I finally recognize the tune to a song I sang with friends on the bus during elementary school field trips:

> *Hey, ho, nobody home,*
> *Meat nor drink nor money have I none,*
> *Yet I will be happy.*

Around the next bend, I overtake the two German girls trooping along with their mother and grandmother singing in their native language. The young ones are in love with the sonorous harmonies created by turning this small verse into an endlessly repeating round. The women are in love with the moment, exchanging smiles over the tops of the children's heads as they return to their car with their bucketful of beach glass. As their voices braid the wind, I hear about the ways life invites us to transcend loss, be happy with nothing, become something else. For the first time all morning, I ride the waves of breath in my chest and re-enter the tide of the world.

EVEN NOW

In Memory of Warren Bruce Zahl
(1957-2013)

ON CHRISTMAS MORNING, I WAKE IN THE SILVERED DARKNESS TO find my brother standing before me. I think it's the light from his dark eyes that has called me out of sleep. He is five years old and wiggling his lively brows, and in his grin some teeth are missing. He has been up a long time already, creeping past the closed doors of the other bedrooms toward the wonder Santa has deposited in our grandparents' living room.

There, past the long-needled pine and the boxy couch, above the cold dark mouth of the fireplace, our bulging felt stockings strain at their thin loops. Bigger boxes and toys form a glorious rubble on the carpet. My brother has been sitting in the pre-dawn chill at a respectful distance from the splendor, hugging his knees, watching as Christmas emerges from the night's shadows.

He can't tell time yet, but he has chosen the perfect moment to pull the aroma of cardboard, cellophane, cap pistols, vinyl dolls, chocolate coins, and candy canes into his lungs and carry it back to where I, the oblivious seven-year-old, still sleep. He lets his gaze hit me like a sunbeam, and as soon as I open my eyes, he lets that caught breath out into the room. There are stirrings, then, in the other bedrooms, and the air is suddenly warm enough to draw us all out from under our grandmother's quilts. Christmas begins as we follow my brother to the glory he has guarded but not yet touched.

These days my house is empty of children who, on Christmas morning, scuffle the last shadows of sleep from a house. But the memory of my brother, as the boy he was, still breathes his blessing at my bedside and lets me know it's time to get up.

HISTORY LESSON

I'VE BEEN RUMMAGING AROUND IN ALREADY FULL CLOSETS LATELY, trying to find space for all the stuff I brought home when I emptied my parents' house last May. It's been rough going, but I stopped wondering why when I realized Mom and Dad lived in their last house for thirty-seven years, only eight years longer than we've lived in ours.

Our youngest son often encounters me staring into space clutching a quilt, wood carving, or photograph. I think my uncharacteristic attempts at organization are making him nervous. "What are you doing? What's that?" he asks.

"Oh, this is some of your Great Aunt Emily's needlepoint," I tell him a little too eagerly. "These are my Barbie clothes, and here are the baby rompers your great grandmother made for your grandfather back in 1925. You wore them once yourself."

I give him these family history updates knowing full well it's drifting in one ear on its way out the other. At twenty-two, he doesn't have a sentimental bone in his body. But as long as he keeps asking, I continue to supply the disregarded answers.

Telling these stories is a kind of test. I'm finding out how much I actually know about the Scotty dog napkin ring, the china baby doll, the anniversary clock, the piece of Native American pottery. If I don't remember what my parents told me about these things, what do they really mean to me?

"It's just stuff," I heard myself say a few months earlier as I watched people carry off Christmas decorations, books, camping gear, and clothing from the garage sale I organized to clear my parents' attic. But I might as well have said, "They're just stories," stories that connect me by an ever-thinning thread to a world that is disappearing.

I remember asking my own mother, "What's that?" and "Who are those people?" whenever I caught her sorting drawers or photographs. I thought I was listening to her explanations, but I didn't retain much. The tiny mirrored powder box with the ostrich puff, that silver thimble—I know they were her mother's, but what about the rest of the story? I'm sure she told me more than once, each time straining to remember what her own mother, dead before I was born, had told her. But it's only now that I understand how the story of an object becomes more precious than the thing itself when there's no one left to ask about it.

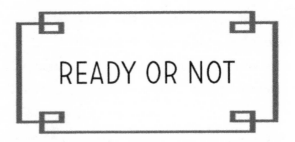

READY OR NOT

A NOTHER SEPTEMBER DAY OVER AND DONE WITH, AND I SPENT all of fifteen minutes outside in it. Here in Sonoma County, the weather is perfect. Morning fog melts into afternoons sweet with heat and long, diamond-cool shadows. Darkness arrives earlier each evening, as if night's reservoir has filled during the summer months and is now spilling over. Every morning, more maple leaves litter my patio and crunch underfoot, releasing the scent of old books, furniture polish, and attic dust. Idly, I wonder if those leaves knew they would fall and what made them let go.

Thoughts like these tell me I am entering my annual season of melancholy, the same one that enveloped me in childhood as I rode my bike alone after school, threading my way through long shadows, anticipating dinner and the clear fires of sunset. As night fell and the big moon rose outside my bedroom window, I wanted autumn to last forever. But these days I hardly look up from my computer or let the golden light stir me in that old way. I am too busy, I tell myself. I'll find time tomorrow, even though

I know it's a lie.

How can it be that as a child I knew enough not to waste the
gift of autumn melancholy? In many ways I was even busier than
I am now. I spent the shortening days getting myself to and from
school, struggling with unwieldy concepts from the cage of my
school desk, struggling harder still on the playground with my
social unease. The afternoons and evenings were filled with music
lessons, chores, homework, and favorite shows on a black-and-
white TV. But I still made time to let the sapphire stillness of fall
live in me. What has changed in my own mind and heart that
allows all this beauty to perish unwitnessed?

Last week, I was in southern California with my mother-in-
law when she was wheeled outside on a gurney for ambulance
transport to a nursing home. The moment the sun touched her
face, she turned toward it, greedily taking its warmth into every
cell. It had been over a month since she had basked in its light,
and I don't know when or if she'll be touched by it again. There
she was, in a smoggy hospital parking lot when she deserved a
cathedral of silence, trees, and sky. I was heartsick thinking of the
poorness of that light, but her face reflected only gratitude as she
received it.

That look should have been the reminder I needed to glory
in autumn's fullness while I can, but no, my season of inattention
persists, along with a belief I did not hold as a child, that time is
something I can afford to waste. Tomorrow, more leaves will drop
on the patio. Another perfect day will be lost.
All this letting go. All this, ready or not

REMEMBERING
THE DECK CHAIR

IT WAS STRANGE, SUDDENLY REMEMBERING THE TEAK DECK CHAIR during my weekly game of wallyball. I'd seen it nearly two weeks earlier at a museum in Halifax as part of an exhibit on the wreck of the *Titanic.* If one of my teammates had asked me about my trip across Canada, I would have never thought to mention the chair, but here it was, occupying my attention when I should have been placing my serve.

Information that lives inside us decides to make itself known at the strangest times. On this recent trip to Canada, during a long day in a rental van, our friend Byron had our group trying to identify poems or part of plays and novels he recited to us. He had dozens in his repertoire, and the more he brought to light, the more he seemed to remember. His efforts inspired us. I found myself delivering snatches of "The Love Song of J. Alfred Prufrock" and Theodore Roethke's "The Bat." Henrietta graced us with some old camp songs. We had Ginny singing standards. Strand us on a deserted island, and before long, we might end up reciting "Hiawatha" in its entirety or adding harmonies to all our old church hymns.

That afternoon Byron posed a question not even he could answer: "What was the housekeeper's name in *Rebecca*?" Unlike some of the obscure lines of Tennyson or Shakespeare he had thrown at us, this was a book most members of the group thought they knew. Suzanne and Norma even remembered the movie and how creepy that so-called servant was. I, of course, was pretty much in the dark about *Rebecca*, even though I'd read the book more than once. Books sustain me, but when it comes to actually remembering their contents, I'm like a baby in its highchair—I'm not comparing last week's peas with tonight's squash. It's all good, mostly. All I really need is something waiting on the end of the spoon.

A few days later, the *Rebecca* question came up again, and suddenly the name "Mrs. Danvers" popped into my head. It was as if a gate opened and a horse called Mrs. Danvers burst out on its race to victory with an announcer screaming its name. The same thing had happened the day before while Henri did the crossword sitting next to me in the train station. Ask me point blank who wrote *Memoirs of a Geisha*, and I would stand outside the fortress of memory forever looking for a way in. But somehow, the crossword clue, worded something like, "Bestseller by William Golden," coupled with the size of the blank that needed filling had me singing the name of the novel like some ecstatic canary.

The sensation of losing information I'm just about to communicate, of being forced to fight my way through the aphasic veil that descends between me and whatever it is I'm trying to relate is curious and sometimes frightening. During that pause in my serve, the memory of the deck chair scavenged from the *Titanic* brought to mind a far greater tragedy set in Halifax. In December of 1917, a French freighter loaded with ammunition collided with another ship in Halifax harbor. The resulting explosion was the largest ever created by humans until Hiroshima. It killed many more people than the sinking of the *Titanic*, and more people than the 9/11 disaster. After contemplating the shipwreck exhibit in Halifax, I'd spent quite a bit of time staring at other museum cases, moved by the displays of personal effects collected from some of the explosion victims— a wedding ring, keys, stubby school pencils, marbles, a worn eraser.

Those images and facts were firmly and radiantly present in my mind during a break between games, so I thought it was a great time to ask my friends if they'd heard of the Halifax Explosion. But as soon as I was called upon to describe the incident, it was as if some demented child had taken a pair of scissors to the fabric of my memory and cut out random words and concepts. I couldn't remember the date of the event and could no more access words like "ammunition" than fly. Scrambling for simple substitutes made me feel like I was in one of those dreams in which I am running, usually from something awful, but getting nowhere. Suddenly, I understood why some people tell the same anecdotes over and over. Maybe they're not stuck in the past; they're just incapable of bushwhacking through new linguistic territory now that the kid with the scissors has gotten to them.

I've often heard brains are like filing cabinets with complex systems of folders and sub-folders available for retrieval when the time is right. My mind is organized, I'm sure of it, but instead of tidy file folders with colorful, easy-to-read tabs, mine is more like my linen closet, with twin bed sheets crammed on the right side of the middle shelf and the queen sheets on the left. I have accumulated more tablecloths and napkins than I could use in this lifetime, and they threaten to spill over from the shelf above that. Easter baskets and Halloween decorations are on the very top behind the sleeping bags. Picnic supplies and extra blankets are stuffed into the closet's nether regions. Generally speaking, I know where things are, but I can never find a pillow case when I need one.

Of course, my linen closet doesn't always look this bad. At least once a year, I pull everything out, refold and stack its contents, and for about two weeks it looks more like the linen closet I imagined for myself when we first moved into this house as newlyweds twenty-six years ago. Back then, our three sets of sheets looked lonely sitting next to the one tablecloth, six napkins, and two extra blankets. There was still plenty of room when we got a pair of sleeping bags a couple of years later. As time went by, this closet became the logical place for my growing collection of antique doilies and tea towels. I'm not sure what prompted me to store the Easter and Halloween decorations there, but by then, God had forbidden me to get rid of anything that might come in handy someday, and now nothing moves in this house without causing major upheaval. And if I moved something, how would I find it again? Around 1982 I relocated the drinking glasses from the cupboard on the right side of the sink to the one on the left, and after all that time, I am sometimes surprised to find stacks of plates when I am looking for a water glass.

So I guess it shouldn't feel odd to be recalling ship wreckage in the middle of a wallyball game. For more than fifty years I've been collecting information the way I keep old keys in a metal cough drops box at the bottom of the drawer by the telephone. They are unlabeled and their locks have long been left behind, but I can't seem to get rid of them. They come to my attention from time to time, unbidden, like a stanza of poetry, the name of a literary villainess, or the image of a lone teak deck chair.

There may be time to acquire better methods of storage and organization. I don't want to become one of those old ladies who gets lost among her newspapers and tuna fish cans, unable to distinguish between what is important and what is best forgotten. But for now, it seems best to appreciate my mind for the deck chairs it brings me, take a deep breath, and play on.

IN TIME

It's nearly December, and I've just now gotten around to putting away the rotary clothesline. It's been months since I've taken the time to peg the laundry that accumulates in the hamper during the week, and no wonder. For me, the clothesline, not the dryer, is the luxury, and requires hours of baking sunshine for its indulgence. Long before I finally decided to wrestle this contraption into winter storage, its outstretched arms had stopped tempting me with the allure of sun-dried sheets and naturally bleached dishtowels. It had become, instead, a skeletal reminder that time is always moving on. I wiped some of the accumulated grime from its aluminum spokes and plastic-coated lines, then collapsed it like a big, backwards umbrella. Afterwards, as storm clouds gathered, I went into the house and tossed some hydrangeas I'd tried to dry in a vain attempt to keep summer's dream alive. Never one to make a clean sweep, I left our Halloween pumpkin on the front porch, even though the neighbors have started in with yuletide decorations.

It's nearly December, and I didn't get the patio chair

cushions stowed before the first big storm of the season. Last night, an atmospheric river from Hawaii, the Pineapple Express, dumped buckets of rain over the house in big, sloppy gusts. I lay awake much of the night listening to the wind howl and imagining it tearing limbs off our fragile old pepper tree, toppling our fences, blowing off the roof of the chicken house. I even went outside during a lull to be sure the hens were safe, causing them to squawk in bleary confusion when I aimed my LED flashlight into the coop. In the morning, I was surprised to see how little had been damaged, that only tattered leaves and small branches littered the yard. As I draped sodden cushions over the wheelbarrow to dry out, I thought about how the world is sometimes stronger than it seems, and I never quite know what to worry about.

It's nearly December, and storm winds have stripped the last of the red and orange leaves from the persimmon tree, revealing the remaining fruit. How seductive those naked persimmons looked held in the highest fingers of the tree, much more mouth-watering than the dozens I've already piled on my dining room buffet, threatening to spoil if I'm not careful. I picked the lower branches early because I didn't want the repeat of last year when something—raccoons, probably—stole everything the night before I planned to harvest, leaving nothing behind but broken riot.

I stretched up to claim the last few within reach. They refused to let go, and I had to wobble on tiptoe, twisting my wrist as if I were fitting the tree with bright orange light bulbs. The tree and I both held on to those last persimmons until I realized this is one task I'm not meant to finish. Soon birds will come in flitting bursts to feast on this bright abundance. They'll peg away at the sweet, softening flesh until the hollowed-out skins hang like washing on a clothesline, all in its perfect order, everything in its own time.

LOOK AGAIN

When we first sense that a pine tree doesn't need us, that it has a physical life and a moral life and spiritual life that is complete without us, we feel alienated and depressed. The second time we feel it, we feel joyful.   —Robert Bly

AT A CURVE OF THE NARROW BLACK RIBBON ROAD LEADING TO the Point Reyes lifeboat station, a line of old cypress trees marches up the grassy hill, part of a straggly windbreak circling the now unoccupied ranger's residence. The trees all carry scars of branches cut or broken, and the pinkish grey bark is so deeply grooved it appears gouged in places. The tree closest to the road shows the most damage: storms have snapped the top limbs and hollows have formed around rotting places. But all this suffering has made the tree a perfect perch for the pair of great horned owls other members of my group have spotted there.

I have yet to see the two owls together. I've also missed the foxes trotting the road with rabbits or voles in their jaws. On this weekend retreat at the lifeboat station, the rarer wonders of the world have revealed themselves to earlier risers and those with calmer hearts. I did see one of the owls and am determined to be satisfied with the way its feathers blended so perfectly with the branch it gripped. With borrowed binoculars I saw the smooth swivel of its head, the luminous yellow eyes boring into mine so intently I believed it had a message for me, even though it turned out to be, "I am not your friend."

Last night at the lifeboat station, my sleep was as thin as the vinyl pad under my sleeping bag. I lay in the dark listening to the wind rattling my bedroom window and to a bird singing somewhere on the nearby hill. If I could think like the wind, nothing in the world would be an obstacle, only forms to move or move past. That thought brought some comfort, but I couldn't get over why a bird would call attention to itself in such a wild place in the middle of the night.

Now, on this sunny summer morning, the hillside looks soft enough to roll down. I know in reality that would hurt like hell, but I stubbornly cling to the dream of doing it. At times like these, I want the lightness of the smaller, chatty birds flitting on the wires near the road, or even the silent efficiency of the pelicans working their big wings over the softly glittering bay to my left. I do not want to be an owl, to hear and feel the wriggling terror that comes with every dinner, to spend my days watchful and still. Up on the hill's crest, I see two hikers who appear to be floating along the trail. Youth and what might be love buoy their steps. If we traded places so they were standing here watching me, I don't think my progress would look effortless to them.

Distance can make things look softer or easier, but distance does not make the owl less formidable. And a tree's indifference is deeper and more complete than the shade spreading beneath its branches. The sky, blue punctuated with the suggestion of clouds, seems to start so far away.

My solitude is interrupted when I meet two of my company standing in the road quietly gazing into the highest branches of the cypress. I look too, hoping to see what they are seeing. I locate the owl from yesterday staring down at us just as something pale flashes in the air beneath its perch. I struggle for a moment to identify it: a feather loosened from its right wing.

And now the feather begins its surprisingly slow descent, the tip of the quill swaying like a pendulum as it drops, describing neat scallops in the air. My eyes, unaccustomed to tracing the movements of the natural world, strain to follow its course. I watch it head straight for me, riding a breeze so steady its flight seems calculated. To receive my gift, I need do nothing more than take one small step off the asphalt and reach up with my right hand. I feel the sky release the feather as my fingers close around it.

LAST WORDS

ON MY LAST DAY THEY WILL COME TO ME, ALL THE WORDS I'VE written—my published work in newspapers, anthologies, and magazines, along with my letters, postcards, and journals. Even my first clumsy poems, the doodled-on high school lecture notes, and florid early diary entries thrown away so long ago will crowd around my bed to murmur their goodbyes. With some occasional confusion and jostling, my writing will come forward, piece by piece, to share a favorite line or two, some brief insight, or a life-changing revelation we experienced in the process of creation. We'll laugh together, cry, or sigh, my words and me, the fragrance of vowels and consonants perfuming the air around my pillow.

This long parade of words will be slow and delicious for me, happening outside the realm of ordinary time. Any of my loved ones keeping vigil might see only the slightest of shadows crossing my face for a few moments. My word-filled communion will remain a mystery to my attendants, but they will still feel oddly comforted. Before they leave my bedside, some of my words will slip into their pockets, climb onto their shoulders or into their warm hair, and go with them where I cannot. My loved ones' dreams will be laced with music that will sound familiar, even if they can't name it. They will catch the scent of gardenias and cinnamon, and those who understood me best will remember that aroma from our last visit on earth.

While a few left behind will cherish some of my writing, even they will lose, destroy, or forget it someday. But the words themselves will live on, as all words written or spoken always do, woven into the fabric of history, notes in the song of time. Even if I forget the words I'm writing now, on my last day they will come to pay their respects. "You'll always live in our hearts," they'll tell me. "We would be nothing without you."

ACKNOWLEDGEMENTS

My heart is full. . .

Many Thanks.

Essays in this collection first appeared whole, in part, in altered form, and occasionally under different titles in the following publications or in stage and radio performances:

"A Little Louder, Please": *Petaluma Argus Courier*, December 2005
        Anderson Valley Advertiser, December 2005
"A Piece of the Pie": *The Kitchen Table*, February, 2009, judihendricks.com
"Bling": *Sitting Room* anthology, 2010;
        Off the Page Readers Theater, 2012
"Boxed In": LiveWire Salon at Zebulon's Lounge, October, 2003
"Breakfast to Go": Page on Stage at the Glaser Center, 2006
"Christmas Day": *Tiny Lights*, 2 (2), 1996
"Couch Fever": Sebastopol Center for the Arts, 2004
"Crab Surprise": *Tiny Lights*, 9 (2), 2003
"Currents": *Speaking of Home*, 1998
"Dance with Me": *Tiny Lights*, 6 (1), 2000
"Driver's Ed": *The Bohemian*, March 3, 2001
"Equal Measure": *Listening In*, 1999
"Even Now": *Petaluma Argus Courier*, December 25, 2002
"Ex Libris": *Tiny Lights*, 5 (2), 1999
"Feast of All Souls": *Tiny Lights*, 8 (2), 2002;
        Writing and Publishing Personal Essays by Sheila Bender, 2005
"Give": *Tiny Lights*, 1 (2), 1995
"Getting a Ride": *Saint Petersburg Times*, May 15, 2005;
Off the Page Readers Theater, 2014
"Glory": *Tiny Lights*, 7 (2), 2001
"Go": *Saint Petersburg Times*, July 11, 2004
"Go Fish": *Expressions II: Seasons*, 2013
"Going Alone": *Tiny Lights*, 11 (2), 2005
"History Lesson": *Tiny Lights*, 15 (1), 2010
"Housebroken": Sebastopol Center for the Arts, November, 2003

"In Passing": *Saltwater, Sweetwater: Women Write from California's North Coast*, Floreant Press, 1998
"In Time": *Tiny Lights*, 18 (1), 2012
"Lost": *Tiny Lights*, 7 (1), 2001
"Lullaby": *Tiny Lights*, 1 (1), 1995
"Mother's Day": *Santa Rosa Press Democrat*, May, 1996;
       Surprise!, The Sitting Room, 2010
"Moving": *Tiny Lights*, 4 (1), 1998
"One Reader's Beginnings": *When I Was A Child I Read . . .*, The Sitting Room, 2013
"Pictures Don't": *Tiny Lights*, 6 (3), 2000
"Ready or Not": *Tiny Lights*, 17 (1), 2011
"Signs of Life": *Tiny Lights*, 3 (1), 1997
"The Anniversary Waltz": *The Dickens*, 2001;
       The Bohemian, February 1, 2001
"The Kingdom of Teacups": *Jasmine Nights and Monkey Pluck: Love, Discovery, and Tea*, Floreant Press/Teacups Group, 2002
"The Other Side of the Fence": *The Dickens*, 2 (1), 1998
"Time Travels": *Tiny Lights*, 9 (1), 2003
"Valentine": *San Francisco Chronicle*, February 9, 1997
"Vision": *Tiny Lights*, 4 (2), 1998
"What Have We Here": *Tiny Lights*, 5 (1), 1999
"Wings": *Tiny Lights*, 14 (2), 2009
"Wounds": *Tiny Lights*, 7 (1), 2001

Resources and Links

Susan Bono: www.susanbono.com
Tiny Lights: A Journal of Personal Narrative:
www.tiny-lights.com
Laurie MacMillan: www.sunfielddesign.com
Rebecca Lawton: www.beccalawton.com
Marlene Cullen: www.thewritespot.us
Ali Cross: Novel Ninjutsu: www.novelninjutsu.com
Doug Fortier: www.dougfortier.com
Sheila Bender: Writing it Real: www.writingitreal.com
Mendocino Coast Writers Conference: www.mcwc.org
Noyo River Review: www.noyoriverreview.org
Petaluma Readers Theatre: www.petalumareaderstheatre.org
Sebastopol Center for the Arts: www.sebarts.org
Aqus Cafè: www.aquscafe.com
Occidental Center for the Arts:
www.occidentalcenterforthearts.org
Copperfield's Books: www.copperfieldsbooks.com
Gallery Bookshop: www.gallerybookshop.com

About the Author

Susan Bono is a writing teacher and freelance editor who edited and published *Tiny Lights: A Journal of Personal Narrative* in print and online at tiny-lights.com from 1995–2014. Her work has appeared in anthologies, magazines, and newspapers, as well as on stage and the radio.

From 2000–2005 she co-coordinated the *Writer's Sampler* series for the Sebastopol Center for the Arts and helped found and co-host the *Speakeasy Literary Saloon* at Petaluma's Aqus Cafè from 2010-2012. She has been a contributing editor for the Pushcart prizes, *Word by Word* on KRCB radio, and for the second edition of Sheila Bender's *Writing Personal Essays: How to Shape Your Life Experiences for the Page*. She's shared her love of personal narrative at writer's conferences, retreats, workshops and literary gatherings all over California.

Susan currently serves on the boards of the Mendocino Coast Writers Conference and Petaluma Readers Theatre, and edits the *Noyo River Review* (noyoriverreview.org). Her two sons, Lucius and Dante, have left the nest, but she's enjoying midlife with her husband and chickens in Petaluma, CA.

www.susanbono.com

p. 10   tee-shirt
p. 16   T-shirt